Tom Quail is a practising family lawyer with over thirty years' experience in this area of law. Tom has provided seminars to other family lawyers, on a range of family law matters and has had articles published in the Journal of the Law Society of Scotland on a regular basis.

Tom is a Solicitor Advocate and Convener of the Law Society Panel accrediting solicitors as Child Law Specialists.

A Practical Guide to Contact and Residence Disputes, Including Remedies, for Family Lawyers in Scotland

A Practical Guide to Contact and Residence Disputes, Including Remedies, for Family Lawyers in Scotland

Tom Quail
Partner and Solicitor Advocate
Wright, Johnston & Mackenzie LLP
LLB (Hons), DipLP NP

Law Brief Publishing

Published 2024 by Law Brief Publishing, an imprint of Law Brief Publishing Ltd
30 The Parks
Minehead
Somerset
TA24 8BT

www.lawbriefpublishing.com

Paperback: 978-1-916698-38-3

PREFACE

Disputes involving children and their welfare whether in relation to residence, contact, non-compliance with a court order, relocation of one parent or wrongful removal of children are notoriously sensitive and difficult to resolve.

Lawyers faced with clients with such problems need to provide their clients with solutions. The book is designed to be a practical aid to assist lawyers in their day to day working lives provide clients with solutions.

As the book is a designed as a practical aid, it is important to cover the significant changes to both the Sheriff Court Rules in family actions introduced September 2023 and how child disputes will be decided once the main provisions of the Children (Scotland) Act 2020 are in force, including the presumption that a child of any age will be capable of forming a view.

I wish to acknowledge the assistance of my colleague Iona Whyte in the chapter relating to Child Abduction.

The law in this book is correct, to the best of my knowledge as at 12th June 2024.

Tom Quail
June 2024

CONTENTS

TABLE OF CASES

CHAPTER ONE

PARENTAL RESPONSIBILITIES AND RIGHTS AND COURT ORDERS

Parental responsibilities and parental rights

The parental responsibilities owed to children and the parental rights enjoyed over children are set out in Sections 1 and 2 of the Children (Scotland) Act 1985 which are as follows:-

1-(1) Subject to section 3(1)(b) and (d) and 3 of this Act, a parent has, in relation to his child, the responsibility –

(a) to safeguard and promote the child's health, development and welfare;

(b) to provide, in a manner appropriate to the stage of development of the child –

(i) direction;

(ii) guidance,

to the child;

(c) if the child is not living with the parent, to maintain personal relations and direct contact with the child on a regular basis; and

(d) to act as the child's legal representative.

2-(1) Subject to section 3(1)(b) and (d) and 3 of this Act, a parent, in order to enable him to fulfil his parental responsibilities in relation to his child, has the right –

(a) to have the child living with him or otherwise to regulate the child's residence;

(b) to control, direct or guide, in a manner appropriate to the stage of development of the child, the child's upbringing;

(c) if the child is living with him, to maintain personal relations and direct contact with the child on a regular basis; and

(d) to act as the child's legal representative.

A child's mother has parental responsibilities and parental rights in relation to a child regardless of whether she is or has been married to the child's father. However, a child's father only acquires parental responsibilities and rights if:-

(1) he is married to the child's mother at the time of the child's conception, or subsequently; or

(2) where not married to the mother at that time or subsequently, the father is registered as the child's father on the child's birth certificate.

These provisions are set out in Section 3 of the 1995 Act.

Provided a child's mother has not been deprived of some or all of the parental responsibilities and rights in relation to a child then the mother, by agreement with the father, can provide that the father will have parental responsibilities and rights in terms of an agreement prescribed in a form by the Secretary of State and registered in the Books of Council and Session. This is set out in terms of Section 4 of the Act.

Court orders relating to parental responsibilities and rights

Section 11 of the Act sets out the orders the court can make in relation to parental responsibilities, parental rights, guardianship or the administration of a child's property.

The orders a court can make are as follows:-

(a) an order depriving a person of some or all of his parental responsibilities or parental rights in relation to a child;

(b) an order imposing upon a person, provided that person is at least sixteen years of age or is a parent of the child, such responsibilities; and giving that person such rights;

(c) an order regulating the arrangements as to (i) with whom; or (ii) if with different persons alternately or periodically, with whom during what periods a child under the age of sixteen years is to live (known as a "residence order");

(d) an order regulating the arrangements for maintaining personal relations and direct contact between a child under that age and a person with whom the child is not, or will not be, living (known as a "contact order");

(e) any order regulating any specific question which has arisen, or may arise, in connection with any of the matters mentioned in paragraphs (a) to (d) above (known as a "specific issue order");

(f) an interdict prohibiting the taking of any steps of a kind specified in the interdict in the fulfilment of parental responsibilities or the exercise of parental rights relating to a child or in the administration of a child's property;

(g) an order appointing a judicial factor to manage a child's property or remitting the matter to the Accountant of Court to report on suitable arrangements for the future, management of the property; or

(h) an order appointment or removing a person as a guardian of a child.

The most frequent and common applications that are made to the court are in relation to residence orders, contact orders and specific issue orders.

Residence and contact orders arise where there is a dispute as to with whom the child is to reside and/or the level of contact that the non-resident parent should enjoy with the child.

Specific issue orders regulate any specific question which arises in connection with parental responsibilities and rights in relation to a child. This is very wide but the most frequent contentious issues relate to the relocation of the child either outwith the jurisdiction or relocation as this would significantly impact on the non resident parent's contact with the child.

Interdicts

The court can make an order prohibiting the taking of any step of a kind specified in the interdict in the fulfilment of parental responsibilities or the exercise of parental rights. In cases involving the relocation of a child, the court are often invited to grant an order for interdict prohibiting the removal of a child from the jurisdiction to permit the court sufficient time to give consideration as to whether a specific issue order permitting relocation is in the interests of the child is to be granted.

Basis for granting any orders relating to children

The legal provisions are set out in Section 11(7) of the Act. In considering whether or not to make any of the orders in terms of Section under Sub-Section 1, the court:-

(a) shall regard the welfare of the child concerned as its paramount consideration and shall not make any such order unless it considers that it would be better for the child that the order be made than that none should be made at all; and

(b) taking account of the child's age and maturity, shall so far as practicable –

   (i) give him an opportunity to indicate whether he wishes to express his views;

   (ii) if he does so wish, give him an opportunity to express them; and

   (iii) have regard to such views as he may express.

In making any decision, the court has to take into consideration factors set out in Section 11(7b) which are:-

(a) the need to protect the child from

   (i) any abuse;

   (ii) the risk of abuse

   which affects, or might affect, the child

(b) the effect such abuse, or the risk of such abuse, might have on the child;

(c) the ability of a person –

  (i) who has carried out abuse which affects or might affect the child; or

  (ii) who might carry out such abuse,

to care for, or otherwise meet the needs of, the child; and

(d) the effect any abuse, or the risk of any abuse, might have on the carrying out of responsibilities in connection with the welfare of the child by the person who has those responsibilities.

In relation to any order the court makes, there are essentially three issues to be considered:-

(a) The Welfare Principle

In considering whether to make an order with respect to a child, and what order to make, the court must regard the child concerned as its paramount consideration.

(b) The Minimum Intervention Principle

In considering whether or not to make an order with respect to a child, the court must not make any such order unless it considers that it would be better for the child if the order were made rather than no order be made.

(c) Views of the Child

In considering whether to make an order with respect to a child and what order to make, the court, taking account of the child's age and maturity must, so far as practicable, give him or her an opportunity to indicate whether or not he or she wishes to express his or her view. If he or she does so wish to express a view, give him or her an opportunity to express them and have regard to such views as he or he may express.

In affording a child an opportunity to make known his or her views, the test is one of practicability including how a child should be given such an opportunity. This very much depends upon the circumstances of each case including the child's age and maturity.

There is a presumption set out in Section 11(10) that a child twelve years of age or more is presumed to be of sufficient age and maturity to form a view. However, in practice we have moved significantly beyond Section 11(10) and essentially have moved to a position whereby there is a presumption that a child of five years or more is of sufficient age and maturity to express a view. The Sheriff Court Ordinary Rules, as amended at 23rd September 2023, sets out that a Form F9 in a child action should be sent to a child where the child is five years of age or more, in the absence of a request to dispense with intimation of the Form F9 on the child and following upon the setting out of reasons why it would be inappropriate to send a Form F9 to a child.

In taking the views of a child, the Sheriff's role is critical. In a family action where a child has returned a Form F9 or otherwise indicated to the court a wish to express a view, then the Sheriff cannot grant any order unless an opportunity has been given for the views of that child to be obtained or heard. The Sheriff must consider whether, and if so, how to seek the child's views. The recording of the views of the child is set out in Rule 33.20. The role of Child Welfare Reporters in seeking the views of the child and undertaking enquiries to assist the court, are emphasised by the amendments to the Sheriff Court Rules (Rule 33.21). Once the provisions of the Children (Scotland) Act 2020 come into force, then the test of practicability will be removed as a child of any age will be presumed to be capable of forming and providing a view. The weight to be given to a child's view will still require to take account of the child's age and maturity.

The procedure in terms of any court applications regarding a child is set out in terms of the Sheriff Court Rules as significantly updated and amended. As from 23rd September 2023, the rules as amended and updated are dealt with in Chapter 5.

Quite often in child disputes the involvement of either new partners, spouses, civil partners becoming involved in the care arrangements and decisions regarding the children are questioned. From a practicable point of view, Section 3(5) of the Act is of assistance in that a parent cannot be with a child all the time and if they arrange for their partner to care for the child, then this is permitted. It allows the partner, at those times, to be essentially in *loco parentis* to fulfil or exercise the parental responsibilities and rights of the parent.

Each dispute in relation to the care arrangements for a child in relation to residence, contact and relocation are decided on what is in the best interests of the child. Whilst it is very much dependent on the circumstances of the case, there are, perhaps, some common principles which require to be borne in mind:-

- As a starting point, contact with both parents does lead to better academic outcomes, better emotional outcomes, lower levels of anxiety and depression for a child;

- Contact still conveys benefits, even where there is conflict;

- Contact is important in relation to self-identity and genealogical connectedness;

- The key role of the resident parent to make contact work or not work probably exceeds anything else currently recognised; and

- It is also essential that any disputes in relation to the care of a child should be determined without delay as the delay itself may well determine the dispute.

CHAPTER TWO

RELOCATION OF CHILDREN

Disputes involving parental rights and child welfare issues, particularly relocation issues are notoriously sensitive and difficult to resolve. As one Judge observed, the main reason is that in most of these cases, there is no right answer. All practical answers are, to some extent, unsatisfactory and therefore, to some extent, wrong and the best that can be done is to find an answer that is reasonably satisfactory.

In this chapter, I am proposing to cover:-

- the legal position;
- comment on the leading and effectively the binding authority of M v M 2012 SLT 428;
- look at a couple of other relocation cases – one of which was successful and the other unsuccessful;
- consider the impact, if any, of the provisions of the Children (Scotland) Act 2020 and
- attempt to draw some common themes from the legislation and case law to give practical advice to a client who wishes to relocate and a client who wishes to oppose a request for relocation.

The law

The law is set out in Sections 2(3) and (6) and Sections 11(2) and (7) of the Children (Scotland) 1995.

Section 2(3) provides that you are not permitted to remove a child habitually resident in Scotland from, or to retain any such child outwith, the United Kingdom without the consent of a person described in subsection (6).

Subsection (6) sets out that is a person (whether or not a parent of the child) who, for the time being has, and is exercising in relation to the child, a right mentioned in paragraph (a) or (c) of subsection (1) above; except that where both the child's parents or person so described the consent required for his removal or retention shall be that of them both. What that means is a person who is exercising parental responsibilities, whether in relation to residence or contact, requires to be consulted and consent provided. In the event that the person does not consent to the relocation, a Specific Issue Order (Section 11(2)(e)) is required prior to relocation.

In such a case in considering whether to make an order (Specific Issue Order) and what order to make, the court:-

(a) shall regard the welfare of the child concerned as its paramount consideration and shall not make any order unless it considers that it would be better for the child that the order be made than that none should be made at all;

(b) taking account of the child's age and maturity, shall so far as practicable:-

  (i) give him an opportunity to indicate whether he wishes to express his views;

(ii) if he does so wish, give him an opportunity to express them; and

(iii) have regard to such views as he may express.

Those sections set out who requires to consent to the proposed relocation. If there is no consent to the relocation, a Specific Issue Order requires to be obtained. Whether that order will be granted or not will depend on what is in the best interests of the child with the child's views being taken account of. If there is an attempt to relocate without the consent of the other parent, then interim interdict should be sought in terms of Section 11(2)(f) of the Act.

M -v- M 2012 SLT 428

This is the leading authority on relocation.

The issue in this case was the weight, if any, which was to be attached to the guidance in the English case of Payne -v- Payne (2001) 2 Weekly Law Reports 1826. The decision in the case of Payne was that, in relation to a relocation case, the most crucial assessment and finding for a Judge (in England and Wales) was the effect the refusal of the application would have on the mother's future psychological and emotional stability.

Facts of the case

Briefly, the couple were married with two children aged seven and five. They separated and had not lived together since 2009. The mother had attempted to move the children to England in 2008 but the father had obtained a court order securing their return to Scotland. It was a fairly fractious dispute. The mother was granted a residence order and remained in the former family home with the children which enabled the father to enjoy regular contact. In 2009, the mother intimated she wished to relocate permanently to England with the children where her present partner lived. The father opposed the move and asked for a residence order in his favour, failing which, variation of the mother's pre-existing residence order to require her to remain in the same area of Scotland. The mother sought a Specific Issue Order to allow her to relocate with the children to England.

The Inner House of the Court of Session decided the following:-

- the guidance in the English case of Payne formed no part of Scots Law;

- a child's welfare was the paramount consideration at all times and that the wishes and interests of either parent had to receive no greater weight than they truly deserved in the circumstances;

- the Sheriff, at first instance, was plainly wrong in failing to satisfy himself that a sufficient level of continuing contact would be achievable; and

- the Sheriff's treatment of the school transition issue was also unsatisfactory to a degree that could not be supported and was inconsistent with the required focus on a child with special needs welfare as the court's paramount consideration.

The court, whilst remitting the matter back to the Sheriff, stated that if the mother's present application was to be renewed then she must undertake the dual burden test imposed by Section 11(7)(a) of the 1995 Act of showing:-

(i) that relocation would actually be in the best interests of the children; and

(ii) that, once again, from the childrens' perspective, it would be better for a Specific Issue Order to be made by the court than for no order to be made at all.

Whilst this is the leading case, other than stating that the child's welfare was the paramount consideration, making reference to insufficient weight being given to the issues of continuing contact and the school transition issue, particularly in light of one of the children having special needs, it does not give a significant degree of guidance as to the factors that a court will take into consideration. It was however clear that there was a significant degree of friction/animosity between the parties as is unfortunately the position in relocation issues. The mother's attempt to move to England without the father's consent did not perhaps assist the mother's case.

MCB -v- NMF 2018 SCLR 660

This is a case where the mother was wishing to relocate with her child to Northern Cyprus.

The facts of the case were as follows:-

- The parties had been in a relationship for some years and lived together for about a year following the birth of their child. At the time of the court hearing, the child was five and a half years old. To preserve her anonymity, the Judge gave her the name Holly. Holly's parents were both Scottish and had lived in Scotland since Holly's birth. Holly's mother wished to move from Scotland to Northern Cyprus where her mother lived, having retired there from Scotland. The father raised the proceedings to prevent Holly's removal to Northern Cyprus.

- The mother asked the court to grant a Specific Issue Order entitling her to remove Holly from Scotland to live in Northern Cyprus and also a residence order. The father opposed both orders and wanted contact regulated between himself and Holly.

- After separation, the mother moved to a property in the same town in the West of Scotland where the parties had lived for many years. Later she moved to another small town about thirty miles away as the school in the other town had particularly high standards.

- The mother had attended college and attained qualifications to work as a medical receptionist but had not been able to secure work in that field. She decided it was best to move to Cyprus and live in her mother's home.

- Since separation, the father had had regular contact with the child, including overnight at the weekend. There had been an incident involving an allegation that the father had collected the child and driven whilst over the limit for alcohol, but a breathalyser test had proved to be negative.

- There were some restrictions before employment could be offered in Cyprus to a foreign national, which included the requirement that the employer had first to attempt to fill the vacancy with a Turkish Cypriot.

- Northern Cyprus was not a signatory to the Hague Convention on the Civil Aspects of International Child Abduction. A court order from the Scottish Jurisdiction in relation to contact arrangements would be neither enforceable nor recognised in Northern Cyprus. Instead, the father would have to apply to the courts in Northern Cyprus; first to be recognised as the child's paternal father and thereafter for access rights.

The central dispute in the case involved comparisons between the child's current circumstances and those in which she would be likely to live in Northern Cyprus. The court considered the following factors:-

- employment prospects;
- accommodation;
- education;
- childcare;
- financial situation;
- family relationships and maintenance of contact and
- environmental factors

The Judge, set out the various relevant factors which she considered, both for and against relocation to Northern Cyprus, but having at the forefront of her mind the need to have Holly's welfare as the paramount consideration. After a proof lasting four days, the Judge concluded that:-

- the child enjoyed a settled life in Scotland where she benefited greatly from close family relationships on both sides;
- she attended an excellent local school and was developing friends and interests independent of her home life in a manner entirely appropriate of her age (five and a half);
- the child's mother, who had been her primary carer since birth, wanted to achieve a better lifestyle for herself and for Holly and her brother. She had an idea that she could do that by moving to Northern Cyprus but failed to prove the existence of a specific job offer;
- the children would require to travel some distance each day if they were to be educated within an English speaking system – the

cost of that English-speaking education would be disproportionately high taking account of the mother's likely earnings, which earnings had not been proved;

- the likely diminution of the strong bond that had developed between Holly and her father was the single biggest factor militating against granting permission to relocate;

- her relationship with her father, which both sides accepted was vital to her, would be reduced to holidays;

- further contact though Skype and similar means of communication was far less satisfactory than physical contact. There was no current pressing need for Holly's relationship with her father to be limited to that;

- the Judge rejected the mother's assertion in her Affidavit that a move to Northern Cyprus was "entirely based around absolute necessity for us" and was of the view that the mother had not yet explored sufficiently the ways in which she could improve her current situation without leaving the country; and

- the child's best interests would be best served by her remaining in Scotland and it could not be concluded that it would be better for the child's mother to have been granted the order which was sought than to make no order at all. The Specific Issue Order was refused.

<u>Donaldson –v- Donaldson 2014 Family Law Reports 126</u>

This is a case in which a Specific Issue Order relating to relocation was granted.

The mother and father separated in June 2010 when the child was aged eleven months. The father had had regular contact, including residential contact until July 2014 when the child went to live in San Francisco with her mother. Since that date, contact had taken place by Skype.

The mother's parents lived in San Francisco. The mother was a US citizen and had no family in Scotland. Her return to the United States was with the permission of the court. The father opposed the request for permission to relocate. At the time, he was completing a PHD at Glasgow University and working part time as an Assistant Warden, tutor and lecturer.

The court appointed a curatrix ad litem who supported the mother's application for permission to relocate but had included craves for continuing contact, including residential contact so long as the child remained in Scotland and after relocation by phone, Skype, contact during school holidays and indirectly by email and weekly progress reports.

The Sheriff having heard evidence over four days decided:-

- the child had a strong bond with both of her parents;
- the father had no tie to Glasgow beyond the completion of his PHD. His father lived in Boston, Massachusetts;
- the father indicated he would be prepared to relocate to the USA if offered employment;
- he would wish to relocate to wherever his daughter was living;

- the mother had offered to apply for a spousal green card in the United States to assist the father in seeking employment in the USA;

- the mother had wished to relocate to San Francisco for two years – she lacked personal support in Scotland and was finding the situation very stressful;

- the child and her mother would be able to live with the mother's parents until she was able to obtain her own accommodation.

- the child would, in that area, be able to attend the same school as the mother had attended when a child;

- the mother had a masters degree in Public Health and intended to pursue a career in Nursing;

- the child was due to start formal education in August 2014; and

- refusal of the mother's application for relocation would be liable to have a significantly detrimental effect on the mother's emotional and mental health from which she would probably not be able to shield her daughter and the detrimental effect on her emotional and mental health would adversely affect her capacity to look after her daughter.

The Sheriff granted a Specific Issue Order. In addition, the Sheriff set out contact whilst the child resided in Scotland and thereafter, following relocation, the contact that would take place whilst she was residing in San Francisco. There clearly was a strong connection with San Francisco.

Common Themes

Relocation is a significant step in any child's life. It is a significant step in an adult's life. It requires, like any significant step, to be carefully thought out and carefully planned. If possible, the parent who will be left behind requires to be engaged in a discussion or, at least, attempts should be made to engage that person in the discussion.

In MCB -v- NMF (the Northern Cypriot case), the first occasion the father found out about the proposed relocation to Northern Cyprus was when he received a letter from the mother's Solicitor explaining she had decided to move to Northern Cyprus. The father in M-v-M had to obtain an order to secure the childrens' return to Scotland when the mother attempted to move to England with them.

If possible, a collaborative approach should be taken. However, that is not always possible, particularly if relationships are already fractured. Matters in such a situation could become more fractious. However, any discussion requires to take account:-

- Accommodation where the children would live;
- the education of the children;
- the employment position on relocation;
- the financial situation albeit, to an extent, that is related to employment; and
- family relationships and maintenance of contact. (Part of the difficulty in the MCB -v- NMF case was the move to Northern Cyprus which was not a signatory to the Hague Convention).

It is clear from the decision in MCB -v- NMF that when it came to accommodation, the education of her children, her employment position and her financial situation, these were not particularly strong factors in favour of relocation. On closer independent analysis, it ought to have been clear that these factors were not particularly strong. This was prior to consideration being given to the significantly reduced level of physical contact between the child and her father. There will obviously be particular circumstances in each case. In the Donaldson case, there were significant ties to the USA and, in particular, San Francisco.

It is important that we stop short of saying there is a presumption against relocation. The focus is squarely on the dual burden test which is imposed by Section 11(7)(a) of demonstrating that:-

- relocation would actually be in the best interests of the children; and

- from the childrens' perspective, it would be better for a Specific Issue Order to be made by the court than by no order to be made at all.

The factors in relation to relocation are not going to be limitless. Whilst there may be certain unusual factors, the issues that were considered in MCB -v- NMF are fairly constant matters.

These are issues which a parent has to consider. However, in considering the issues, there has to be very much focused on what is best for their children as opposed to what is best for the parent.

It is important to stress that in relocation cases, the dual burden is a high bar and making strenuous collaborative steps to engage the other parent is a significant factor. Parents have to be mindful of their responsibilities as set out in Section 1 of the 1995 Act. There is an obligation to be a responsible parent and you have to act responsibly, which is doing what is best for your children as opposed to what is best for you.

CHAPTER THREE

NON-COMPLIANCE WITH CONTACT AND RESIDENCE ORDERS

The remedy of asking the court to make a finding of contempt of court for non-compliance with a court order, normally contact is a remedy of last resort. It is an invitation to the court to make a finding that one parent has not complied with an order of court. It is an extreme remedy.

It is important to stress that, despite what the view of the client is, not every occasion when an order for contact is not complied with is contempt of court.

Contempt of court is:-

> *"The name given to conduct which challenges or affronts the authority of the court or the supremacy of the law itself, whether it takes place in or in connection with civil or criminal proceedings". (HM Advocate v Airs 1975 JC 64 at page 69)*

> *"The offence of contempt of court is an offence sui generis and when it occurs it is within the province of the court to punish it under its power...to take effective action to vindicate its authority and preserve the due and impartial administration of justice".*

Prior to going down the route of endeavouring to obtain a finding for contempt, it is important to explore alternatives and other options. If you attempt to resolve issues other than through court procedure, and if you then have to ultimately go down the legal route, it strengthens the argument which you are making to the court, namely that you have exhausted all other remedies and that you are able to demonstrate that the remedy you are seeking is the only option which is available to the court. You have a duty to the client and the court to explore and exhaust all other reasonable options. NJDB -v- JEG (2012) UK SC 21 reminds us that there is a duty on both Counsel and Solicitors to focus on the matters of the most immediate significance, namely on the child or the children.

When acting for a client who is not seeing his or her children, the client, despite what can be a difficult and upsetting time, has to be calm, measured and reasonable. You as a solicitor have to ensure that a client conducts himself or herself in this manner.

Your client has to act in accordance with your instructions. It is essential that the focus should be, and remains, on the conduct of the individual who is not complying with an order of court. Any deviation from calm, measured and reasonable behaviour on the part of your client will deflect attention away from the benefit / position you are trying to secure on his or her behalf – you have to remain in control of your client.

The Standard Expected of a Parent in Contact Disputes

It is helpful to look at what is expected of a parent in complying with a court order. It appears that the following points are relevant:-

- The Children (Scotland) Act 1995, Section 1(1)(b)

    - In the context of a contact order, a parent (with care) has a responsibility to provide, in a manner appropriate to the stage of the development of the child, direction and guidance.

- Section 3(4) of the 1995 Act provides;-

- The fact that a person has parental responsibilities or parental rights in relation to a child shall not entitle that person to act in a way which would be incompatible with any court order.

- Accordingly, if there is a conflict between the discharging of responsibilities as a parent and complying with a court order then compliance with the court order takes precedence / priority.

• Section 11(7)(a) of the 1995 Act is relevant in that when there is an order for contact made, it follows that the court has made a determination that it considers it is better for the child or children that the order for contact be made than that none should be made at all. It is not a given that an order for contact is automatically granted. This is even more so taking account of the abuse and cooperation provisions introduced in 2006 which is set out in Section 11(7)(b) to (d) of the 1995 Act. The effect of abuse or risk of abuse are relevant factors in making an order for contact under Section 11(7)(a). Accordingly, on the basis that there is a court order for contact then it follows that that order should be complied with.

Whilst that is the legislative provisions, what are the views of the court?

These are as set out in two court decisions:-

Blance v Blance 1978 SLT 74

The mother in this case was granted access (contact), which was not taking place. In deciding what was expected of a parent who had custody (residence), the court made certain observations which are as relevant today as they were in 1978:-

- It is unfortunate if parents are not aware of what an order allowing access involves.

- When complaints are made about such an order not being obtempered, it is frequently said that the child in question would not go, or did not want to go. The court accepted that it cannot be in the best interests of any child to be physically coerced or compelled to accompany a parent if that child resolutely persists in refusing to do so. On the other hand, the parent or person who has custody or actual control of the child does not fulfil his obligations by merely leaving it to the child's decision whether or not to go with the person to whom a right of access has been granted.

- The best interests of the child may inevitably involve some temporary upset and the whole purpose of the court awarding access would be frustrated if the effect of the decision were to be handed over to the child. The child should be persuaded, encouraged and instructed, but not physically forced to go with the person to whom access has been granted.

- In this particular case, when the former wife arrived to collect the children the husband said *"All those that want to go put their coats on"*. Not surprisingly, the Judge did not consider that as sufficient persuasion, encouragement or instruction.

The second case is Brannigan v Brannigan 1979 SLT, Notes of Recent Decisions page 73

The Pursuer argued that the children did not wish to see the Defender, their father.

The Judge in that case indicated:-

- *"The mother's technique was simply to leave it to these young children to make a decision for themselves which was much too important to leave to them without positive guidance and genuine encouragement".*

The Judge then went on:-

- *"This attitude was reflected in the difficulties which she created for the father in his desire to see the children and in particular her failure to invite him into her house when he called with presents for them. If she had shown any real interest in seeing that the children did not lose touch with their father I have little doubt that a healthy attitude on the part of the children towards their father could readily have been fostered".*

The Judge in the Brannigan case explained that what the mother ought to have done was clearly explained in the Blance case.

Whilst these two cases were decided in 1978 and 1979 the role of the parent with custody (residence) was and is very important in ensuring that access operated well.

Prior to making any order for residence/contact, the court will have taken account of the views of the child in complying with the provisions of Section 11(7)(b) of the 1995 Act. However, the role of the resident parent is key and, in particular, the capacity of the resident parent to make contact work or not work exceeds anything currently recognised.

Looking at the Act, the standard expected of a parent with care would appear to be one of providing to his/her children in an issue of contact:-

- direction;

- guidance;

- persuasion;
- encouragement; and
- instruction.

Judicial Views on Non-Compliance with Contact Orders

A client who is faced with:-

- a parent who is not prepared to provide the appropriate direction, guidance, persuasion, encouragement and instruction;
- the ongoing costs of litigation;
- a court/Judge/Sheriff that is unable to secure compliance with the court order; and
- the upset and the distress which it is visibly causing his children as well as himself

then, not surprisingly, and regrettably, quite often, a parent faced with all of these obstacles and difficulties may simply give up on his relationship with his children.

The courts, in particular the Court of Session, have taken a firm view in relation to failure to comply on the part of, predominantly the resident parent, with orders for contact. These decisions demonstrate that the court will take appropriate steps to ensure that contact and other family orders are complied with.

The decisions also provide guidance to us as practitioners when advising our clients of the consequences of non-compliance with an order of court.

There are three cases of relevance.

TAM v MJS [2009] Court of Session Inner House page 44

In this case, TAM raised an action for declarator that he was the father of MJS's child, born 2001 and for contact. The action commenced on 15th of September 2005. An action for declarator was granted and a contact order was made. The mother, MJS, prevented contact taking place as much as possible. After a number of court hearings (predominantly Child Welfare Hearings which did not result in contact taking place), there was a Motion to ordain the mother to appear on 13th of December 2007 to explain her failure to comply with the contact order. The mother, MJS, was found in contempt on 5th of March 2008. After further procedure, as a result of the mother's conduct, she was imprisoned on 16th of December 2008 for a period of three months.

In the interim, MJS had also given birth to a child in September 2008.

On 19th of December 2008, having given an undertaking to comply with the order for contact, she was released from prison by way of interim liberation. In the period between 19th December 2008 when MJS was granted interim liberation and 15th May 2009 when the court made a final order, despite the undertaking given by MJS to the court, contact did not take place.

On 15th May 2009, three and half years after the action commenced in September 2005, the court upheld the original penalty of three months civil imprisonment. In addition, the court also found that the undertaking given by MJS to the court on 19th December 2008 was a material factor leading to the granting of interim liberation on 19th December 2008 and as the undertaking had not been complied with then the breach of that undertaking also was a contempt of court.

When the action was raised in September 2005 the child was four years and ten months. By May 2009 the child was eight and a half. This was the type of delay that was highlighted by the court in NJDB -v- JEG (2012) UK SC 21 and, as a consequence of which, in the Sheriff Court, case management for Section 11 orders was introduced for actions raised after 3rd June 2013, the purpose of which was to narrow the issues in dispute and restrict the scope of any hearing.

The following points from the court's decision are of relevance:-

- MJS had disregarded the consistent advice of a succession of solicitors.

- The worst aspect of the case was that in order to deprive the father of contact, MJS had made grave and serious allegations against him.

- In a case of this kind, there was the special consideration that a sentence of imprisonment separates the children from the primary carer. The court said that consideration is relevant but not paramount. The court must uphold the rule of law and protect the interests of the innocent party. Whilst the court must be mindful of the effect of a separation of a mother and child, it is entitled nonetheless to impose a sentence of imprisonment if the circumstances warrant it. The court was of the view that the circumstances in this case warranted it even although MJS had another child who was eight months old at the time she was imprisoned.

- The court saw no reason why they should recall the sentence. If they did recall the sentence, it would encourage MJS in the view that it is for her to decide which orders of the court she would obey. It would undermine the authority of the Sheriff and deprive the father of his rights. In effect, it would perpetrate an injustice at their own hands.

The conduct of MJS was extreme – as was the sentence imposed.

AG v JB [2011] CSIH 56

The action was raised in February 2006 by the father of a child who was born on the 20th of January 2005 seeking parental rights and responsibilities and an order for contact.

- On the 10th April 2007 (after a Proof), the father was granted an order for contact.

- After significant further procedure, mainly Child Welfare Hearings at which the mother failed to appear, on 28th September 2009 a Proof took place at which the mother, once again, failed to appear having sent a letter to the court saying she would not attend.

- The Sheriff heard evidence from the father and the father's Solicitors who gave evidence that the mother who was not represented had informed him repeatedly that she would never agree to contact taking place.

- On 4th November 2009, the mother was found to be in contempt of court and sentenced to two months civil imprisonment.

- Following upon the mother on 13th November 2009 providing an undertaking to comply with the court order for contact, the mother was released from custody on an interim basis.

- After further significant court procedure which comprised mostly of the mother

  (a) giving assurances that contact would take place and

  (b) not attending court hearings,

the Court of Session issued a decision on 13th July 2011, upholding the decision of the Sheriff on the 4th November 2009 to find the mother in contempt and sentencing her to a two months period of civil imprisonment.

The court in that case said:-

> *"This case exemplifies yet another attempt by a custodial parent to sever the bond between the other parent and their child by means of delaying tactics and in due course by protracted defiance of an order of court. This court has already made clear its disapproval of such conduct".*

The court made special reference to the TAM v MJS decision.

Accordingly, in the circumstances, if there is conduct on the part of the parent with care in not complying with a court order, then the remedy of inviting to court to make a finding that one parent had not complied with an order of court, namely a finding of contempt, albeit an extreme remedy, is open to the non-resident parent.

CM -v- SM 2017 SC 235

This is a case worth looking at as it follows the procedure that was adopted as a consequence of allegations or complaints of non-compliance with a contact order. It is a decision of the Extra Division of the Court of Session and accordingly carries significant weight.

In January 2010, a father brought proceedings seeking contact orders in relation to his child who, at the time, was one year old having been born in January 2009. In the course of the contact proceedings, the court made certain interim contact orders. The father complained in October 2010 initially that the mother had committed contempt of court by wilfully refusing to allow contact on a number of occasions in accordance with the orders.

In March 2011, the court ordered parties to lodge a Minute and Answers in relation to the allegations of contempt. In due course, a hearing was fixed to deal with both the contact action and the contempt proceedings together. Following further procedure, the hearing (proof), both in relation to the contact action and contempt, did not start until 10th January 2013. By that point, the father had added further allegations to the contempt proceedings; although the mother had not answered them. The hearing lasted for seven days between 10th January and 8th August, both 2013.

The case had been allocated to a temporary (part time) Sheriff. On the second last day of the hearing, the mother's agent moved the court not to proceed with the contempt proceedings any further. The mother's legal agent argued that to hear both matters together was incompetent. It was argued on behalf of the mother that she would be prejudiced because she could not decline to give evidence in the contempt proceedings while giving evidence in the contact action. The Sheriff refused that Motion. The Sheriff proposed and suggested that the mother could, in the court proceedings, indicate whether she was electing to give evidence in both proceedings or not.

On 24th October 2013, the Sheriff found the mother in contempt in respect of five separate occasions of refusal to allow contact. The Sheriff deferred sentence on a number of occasions between 17th November 2013 and 20th May 2015.

On 20th May 2015, the Sheriff imposed a three-month custodial sentence on the mother in respect of her contempt. In doing so, the Sheriff took into account subsequent incidents of non-compliance with the court order such as the mother refusing to allow access to Social Workers and subsequent conduct in the contact action.

The mother appealed to the Court of Session arguing that the procedure adopted in hearing both the contact and contempt proceedings together was inappropriate, it afforded an opportunity for substantial injustice to be done, further the mother had suffered a miscarriage of justice as a result of defective representation. In any event, the sentence imposed was excessive and took into account irrelevant considerations such as the mother's subsequent attitude to contact.

The court decided that:-

- The issues to be resolved in the contempt proceedings and the contact action were quite different;

- It would seldom be appropriate for the issue of contempt to be dealt with in the substantive action i.e contact to which the alleged contempt was ancillary;

- Doing so was likely to delay resolution of the dispute and cause confusion and uncertainty as had occurred in the present case;

- The Sheriff's decision in this case to hear the contempt proceedings at the same time as the contact action or proof in the contact action was wrong in principle;

- The court indicated that it had long been established that contempt of court is an offence sui generis HM Advocate – Airs (page 69) but it has characteristics which, in many cases, make it quite a criminal in nature. The contempt must be proved to the criminal standard beyond reasonable doubt. The alleged contemnor is not a compellable witness and perhaps, more importantly, a finding of contempt may result in a fine or period of imprisonment. For those reasons, it is important that the procedure adopted enables the alleged contemnor to know exactly what is alleged against him or her, to obtain legal advice and to give clear instructions to those acting;

- Furthermore, the issue in this case, namely refusal to facilitate contact, is all that requires to be proved unless it is admitted. All that needs to be proved in such a case is that the court made an order for contact, that contact did not take place in accordance with that order and that failure resulted from wilful disobedience whereas, by contrast, the issues in a contact action will be quite different as enquiry will focus on what is in the best interest of the children;

- There was force in the argument that the procedure adopted in the hearing in both matters together had afforded an opportunity for substantial injustice to be done, the device of asking the mother to elect whether she wanted to give evidence in the contact action only or also in respect of the contempt proceedings did not overcome the prejudice. There was a difficulty in allowing the two very different types of proceedings to be heard together. It might be almost impossible for the Sheriff to make findings according to different standards of proof and very difficult not to allow impressions of the witnesses in evidence on some matters to infect thinking on the other matter;

- The issue of a possible custodial sentence was a factor requiring that contempt proceedings should be dealt with in short compass;

- The sentence had been excessive, the delay of over a year a half between the finding of contempt and sentencing was inimical to justice, the reference to events other than the five instances of established contempt were irrelevant to the question of sentencing; a custodial sentence, particularly in a mother with whom the children live, should only be imposed with reluctance and as a last resort. Without taking into account the subsequent events, it was excessive to impose a custodial sentence of any length and the appeal, both in relation to the findings and the sentence, was allowed.

In this case, it took between 20th October 2010 and 15th May 2015 to find that there were five instances of contempt, only two of which (8th October 2011 and 7th April 2012) had been answered.

Accordingly, looking at these three decisions it is clear that the court takes a less tolerant view of the small number of individuals who are determined not to comply with court orders and to apply the appropriate sanction for what amounts to a failure on the part of a parent to discharge her legal responsibility and comply with an order of court.

However, it is important that the appropriate procedural matters are attended to, otherwise, consequences such as arose in CM -v- SM will occur. Regrettably, in the CM -v- SM, the concerns and complaints that the father had in relation to the mother regarding non-compliance with orders with contact were never addressed due to the defective procedure adopted by the Sheriff. The child was aged one (born in January 2009) when proceedings were raised and aged eight by the time the Inner House issued its decision.

In the next chapter, we consider contempt of court procedure/action.

CHAPTER FOUR

CONTEMPT OF COURT PROCEEDINGS

On the basis that all other avenues to resolve issues have been exhausted then we are left with the remedy of inviting the court to make a finding that a parent who has not complied with an order of court is in contempt of court. How you go about this would appear to me to be as follows:-

1. Initially, you have to establish contempt of court. For the purposes of this discussion, contempt of court includes:-

    - A failure to obtemper or comply with an order of court; and/or

    - Breach of an undertaking given to the court; and/or

    - An abuse of the court process.

2. To be in contempt of court the conduct or omission has to be:-

    - Wilful or intentional; or

    - Inexcusably careless; or

    - In flagrant disregard of the due course and administration of justice.

3. The standard of proof required to establish contempt is beyond reasonable doubt.

Accordingly, a finding of contempt is not an easy test to establish.

The guidelines in relation to the procedure for contempt are set out in Macphail Sheriff Court Practice in the 4th Edition, paragraphs 2.18 to paragraph 2.25. The case of CM -v- SM 2017 SC 235 is also helpful in that it sets out that the proceedings for contempt should be by way of Minute for Contempt and Answers.

4. As in any court procedure, there has to be a potential benefit or a purpose to the client in taking proceedings.

5. The client who is a parent has a legal responsibility to his or her children. If one parent is behaving unreasonably or irresponsibly then it is all the more important that the parent who is complying with the court order conducts himself reasonably and responsibly. The parent has a legal obligation to do so – the direction and guidance responsibility is set out in terms of section 1 of the 1995 Act.

   The benefits of contact (better academic and emotional outcomes, lower levels of anxiety and depression, contact particularly important for boys with their father, importance of self-identity and genealogical connections) are well established.

   Accordingly, ensuring that children see their father is for the benefit of the children and any benefit to the father has to be viewed as a secondary benefit. The court will only make an order for contact if it is in the interest of the child as the child's welfare is of paramount consideration (Section 11(7)(a) of the 1995 Act).

6. Whilst that is all very well meaning, the three cases in the previous chapter demonstrate that these are costly proceedings for the client in terms of finance, time and emotional energy.

7. Looking at the financial position, it is important that the financing of contempt court procedure, like any other court procedure, is addressed, whether this has to be on a private basis or through sanction from the Legal Aid Board.

8. The client also has to be prepared to make a commitment in terms of time and be emotionally able to take this process to a conclusion.

9. The procedure in relation to contempt is by way of a Minute.

10. There has to be averments of:-

    i) the court order; and

    ii) non-compliance with the court order.

The averments should be specific, relevant and concise. The averments should take into consideration the standard expected of a resident parent, namely persuading, providing guidance, instruction, encouragement and direction and demonstrate that there has been a failure to meet that standard. At the end of the various averments in the Minute, there should be a plea in law to the effect that the non-compliant party should be ordained to appear before the court to explain the failure to comply with the specific court order and, failing the provision of an explanation which is satisfactory to the court, to make a finding for contempt as a result of the non-compliance with the court order. The averments should be in short compass. All that needs to be proved in such a case is that the court made an order for contact, that contact did not take place in accordance with that order and that that failure resulted from wilful disobedience.

11. As the course of conduct referred to in the Minute will be over a period of time, certainly at least a few months, it would be

beneficial if the client retains and provides to you diary notes of how contact operates or not on each occasion.

12. It is also important that the court assigns a separate case reference number to the Minute procedure from the original action.

13. In advising the client as to what you information he requires to provide, it is helpful to bear in mind that competing versions of events are seldom of much importance in guiding future contact decisions. The client should focus on what the court order is and why the mother/father has not complied with the court order. The client should be requested to report and not give an opinion. It may be that, if the reports he provides are factually accurate, they could possibly be lodged as productions. If the reports or notes contain commentary or opinions then they cannot.

14. When the Minute initially calls in court, if the averments or the conduct is/are denied then there should be an order for Minute and Answers and a Proof/final hearing fixed.

    i) In the time period between the Minute originally calling and the final hearing Proof, there will be an opportunity to adjust the Minute and Answers. That is an opportunity which should be taken.

    ii) Bearing in mind that the period between the Minute calling and the Proof / final hearing could be a few months it is important to monitor the compliance or non-compliance with the original court order in that period and adjust the pleadings to ensure that they are current and accurate.

15. Thereafter, preparations can be made for the final hearing / Proof, which is effectively just like a normal civil Proof i.e.

citing of witnesses, productions etc bearing in mind the higher standard of proof. It is also important to take into consideration that the contempt proceedings should be in short compass and dealt with swiftly.

16. If at the end of the Minute procedure the grounds are either admitted or established and the sheriff or judge makes a finding of contempt, it is then for the court to impose sanctions.

17. The period between lodging a Minute for Contempt and a hearing/determination should be short in view of a custodial sentence being a possible penalty.

18. It may well be that once the Minute procedure is instigated this may achieve a resolution prior to a final hearing or determination by the court. It is important to bear in mind that the purpose of the Minute procedure is to ensure compliance with the court order which is for the benefit for the child. The contempt procedure is not intended to punish the person who is not complying with the court order. The issuing of penalties or punishments is the preserve of a Judge or sheriff.

19. If there is a difficulty with compliance with a court order an option to consider is a change in the arrangements for residence of the child if it would be better. A finding of contempt demonstrates that the mother/father is not prepared to comply with a contact order and would form part of the arguments for a change of residence.

CHAPTER FIVE

SHERIFF COURT RULES IN RELATION TO FAMILY ACTIONS

The Family Law Committee of the Scottish Civil Justice Counsel undertook research to identify areas for improvement, particularly on preventing undue delay in proceedings relating to the welfare of children. This followed upon the significant criticism that was set out by the Supreme Court in relation to Sheriff Court procedure in NJDB -v- JEG 2012 UK SC 21. The Ordinary Cause Rules in relation to family actions, which are set out in Chapter 33 were, as a consequence, amended. The new rules relate to Actions and Minutes to Vary lodged on or about 25th September 2023.

The changes introduced by the new rules include:-

- Chapters 9 and 10 of the Ordinary Cause Rules no longer apply to family actions. The relevant provisions are accommodated within the new Chapters 33 and 33A. This makes matters simpler and provides procedural clarity for family cases. The case management provisions set out in the rules apply to all family and civil partnership actions and anticipate that with greater judicial case management this will result in cases being resolved more quickly; and

- Options Hearings have been replaced with an Initial Case Management Hearing and a Full Case Management Hearing. The hearings will have a checklist and parties will be expected to advise the court about each matter. The intention is to ensure that the important issues are clearly focused so that cases can be resolved more quickly and reduce system churn with fewer continuations.

It might be helpful to look at the Chapter 33 rules in relation to actions where Section 11 orders are being sought.

Rule 33.3 – Averments where Section 11 orders sought

Where a Section 11 order under the Children (Scotland) Act 1995 is being requested in respect of a child, then there is a requirement to include:-

(a) particulars of any proceedings known which are continuing whether in Scotland or elsewhere and which relate to the child in relation to which a Section 11 is sought or the parents of that child;

(b) an averment that no permanence order (as defined in Section 80(2) of the Adoption and Children (Scotland) Act 2007) is in force in respect of the child.

Rule 33.7A – Warrant and forms for intimation to a child and for seeking a child's view

In an action where a Section 11 order is being requested in respect of a child who is not a party to the action, the requirements are:-

(a) to include in the Initial Writ a crave for warrant for intimation on the seeking of the child's views in Form F9; and

(b) when presenting an Initial Writ for warranting, submit a draft Form F9 showing the details that a Pursuer proposes to include when the form is sent.

Where it is considered that it would be inappropriate to send the Form F9 to the child (eg. where the child is under five years of age), the Pursuer has to include in the Initial Writ:-

(a) a crave to dispense with intimation and the seeking of the child's views in the Form F9; and

(b) averments setting out the reasons why it is inappropriate to send the Form F9 to the child.

The Sheriff requires to be satisfied that the draft Form F9 has been drafted appropriately. The Sheriff may dispense with intimation and the seeking of the views in the Form F9 or make any other order that the Sheriff considers appropriate.

Rules 33.19, 19A, 19B, 19C and 19D – Views of the child

These rules set out the procedure for sending the Form F9 to the child which are as follows:-

Section 11 Order sought by the Pursuer – Undefended Action Rule 33.19

In an undefended action, the Pursuer requires:-

(i) on expiry of the period of notice, to send the child a Form F9 that was submitted and approved under Rule 33.7A;

(ii) lodge with the Minute for Decree a Certificate of Intimation in Form F9A; and

(iii) not send the child a copy of the Initial Writ.

Unless there are particular circumstances, the Sheriff cannot grant Decree in the twenty-eight day period following the date in which the Form F9 was sent to the child.

Section 11 order sought by Pursuer – Rule 33.19A – (b) views of the child defended actions

In a defended action in which only the Pursuer is seeking a Section 11 order and warrant has been granted for intimation and the seeking of the child's views in Form F9, the Pursuer must:-

(i) no later than 14 days after the Notice of Intention is lodged, send the child the Form F9 that was submitted and approved;

(ii) on the same day, lodge a Certificate of Intimation, in Form F9A; and

(iii) not send the child a copy of the Initial Writ, the Notice of Intention to Defend or the Defences.

Section 11 order sought by Defender – Rule 33.19B

In a defended action in which only the Defender only is seeking a Section 11 order and warrant has been granted for intimation and the seeking of the child's views in Form F9, the Defender must:-

(i) no later than 14 days after the Notice of Intention is lodged, send the child the Form F9 that was submitted and approved under Rule 33.34;

(ii) on the same day, lodge a Certificate of Intimation in Form F9A; and

(iii) not send the child a copy of the Initial Writ, the Notice of Intention to Defend or the Defences.

Section 11 order sought by both Pursuer and Defender – Rule 33.19C

Where Section 11 orders are sought by both the Pursuer and the Defender, and warrant has been granted for intimation and the seeking of the child's views in the Form F9, then the Pursuer must:-

(a) no later than 14 days after the Notice of Intention is lodged, send the child the Form F9 that was submitted and approved under Rule 33.7A, amended so as also to narrate the Section 11 order sought by the Defender;

(b) on the same day, lodge a Certificate of Intimation, in Form F9A and send the Defender a copy of the Form F9 that was sent to the child; and

(c) not send the child a copy of the Initial Writ, the Notice of Intention to Defend or the Defences.

Views of the child – the Sheriff's role – Rule 33.19D

In a family action, in relation to any matter affecting a child where the child has:-

(a) returned a Form F9 to the Sheriff Clerk; or

(b) otherwise, indicated to the court a wish to express views,

the Sheriff must not grant any order unless an opportunity has been given for the views of that child to be obtained or heard. Prior to hearing the views of the child, the Sheriff must consider whether, and if so how, to seek the child's views in advance of making the order.

Where a child has indicated their wish to express views, the Sheriff must order any steps to be taken that the Sheriff considers appropriate to obtain or hear the views of that child.

A Sheriff cannot grant an order in a family action in relation to any matter affecting a child who has expressed views unless the Sheriff has given due weight to the views expressed by that child, having regard to the child's age and maturity.

In an action where a Section 11 is being requested, where the Form F9 has either not been sent to the child or where it has been sent and the Sheriff considers the passage of time requires it to be sent again, the Sheriff may order either party to:-

(a) send the Form F9 to the child within a specified timescale; and

(b) on the same day, lodge a copy of the Form F9 that was sent to the child and a Certificate of Intimation in Form F9B.

Unlike Rule 33.19A, B and C, there does not appear to by any requirement to send a copy of the Form F9 to the other party. However, this could be addressed by this being dealt with by way of a verbal Motion.

Recording of views of the child – Rule 33.20

Where a child expresses a view on a matter affecting, and whether expressed personally to the Sheriff or to a person appointed by the Sheriff for that purpose, or provided by the child in writing, the Sheriff, or the person appointed by the Sheriff, shall record the views of the child in writing and the Sheriff may direct that such views and any written views given by a child shall:-

(a) be sealed in an envelope marked "views of the child – confidential.";

(b) be kept in the court process without being recorded in the Inventory of Process;

(c) be available to a Sheriff only;

(d) not be opened by any person other than a Sheriff; and

(e) not form a borrowable part of the process.

Child Welfare Reporters – Rule 33.21

This rule contains detailed provisions as to the role of Child Welfare Reporters in seeking the views of the child and/or undertaking enquiries to assist the court.

At any stage in a family action in relation to any matter affecting a child, the Sheriff can appoint the Child Welfare Reporter:-

(a) to seek the views of the child and to report any views expressed by the child to the court; or

(b) undertake enquires and report to the court.

A Child Welfare Reporter may only be appointed if the Sheriff is satisfied that:-

(a) it is in the best interest of the child; and

(b) it will promote the effective and expeditious determination of an issue in relation to the child.

When a Child Welfare Reporter is appointed, the interlocutor must:-

(a) specify a date by which the report is to be submitted to the court;

(b) include a direction as to the fees and outlays of the Child Welfare Reporter. The direction in the interlocutor must assign liability for payment of the Child Welfare Reporter's fees and outlays and require that liability to be borne in equal shares or by one or more parties to the action on such other basis as may be justified on cause shown;

(c) where the appointment is seeking the views of the child and reporting any views expressed by the child to the court, the interlocutor requires to specify the issues in respect of which the child's views are to be sought and include a direction as to whether a copy of the report is to be provided to the parties;

(d) where the appointment is to undertake enquiries and to report to the court, the enquiries to be undertaken requires to be specified and the issues requiring to be addressed in the report; and

(e) where the appointment is seeking both the views of the child and to report any views to the court, and also to undertake enquiries and report to the court, then there requires to be a direction as to whether the views of the child should be recorded in a separate report and, if so, whether a copy of that report is to be provided to the parties.

It is normally the case that when the court order is issued, the issues or the enquiries to be undertaken by the Child Welfare Reporter are specified in an annex to the interlocutor in a Form F44.

The interlocutor will specify the date the report requires to be lodged with the court which will be no less than three clear days before the Child Welfare Reporter.

The Sheriff Clerk, on the issuing of an interlocutor appointing a Child Welfare Reporter, must provide to the Child Welfare Reporter:-

(1) a certified copy of the interlocutor; and

(2) sufficient information to enable the Child Welfare Reporter to contact the Solicitors for each party of the proceedings, or any party not represented by a Solicitor.

The Child Welfare Reporter must send the report to the Sheriff Clerk by the date specified in the interlocutor and, unless otherwise directed, send a copy of the report to each party to the proceedings by that date.

There are ancillary provisions for further directions being given by the Sheriff and for the Child Welfare Reporter bringing to the attention of the Sheriff Clerk any impediment to the performance of the carrying out the report, and for providing the Child Welfare Reporter with copies of such documents lodged in process as may be specified and provide further directions to the Child Welfare Reporter.

Referral to Family Mediation – Rule 33.22

In an action where parental responsibilities or rights is an issue, the Sheriff may, at any stage of the action where the Sheriff considers it appropriate, refer that issue to a Mediator accredited to a specified family mediation organisation.

In deciding whether to do so, the Sheriff must have particular regard to any averments of domestic abuse when considering the appropriateness of referring the action or an issue in the action to mediation.

Specified family mediation organisations are CALM (Comprehensive Accredited Lawyer Mediators) through the Law Society and Mediators accredited through Family Mediation Scotland.

Child Welfare Hearing – Rule 33.22A

This sets out the rules in relation to the fixing and the hearing of a Child Welfare Hearing.

Application for order to disclose whereabouts of children – Rule 33.23

If the whereabouts of children are not known, then an application can be made under Section 33(1) of the Family Law Act 1986 for the disclosure. The Sheriff can order the person against whom the order has been made to appear before him or to lodge an Affidavit.

Defended family actions – Initial and full Case Management Hearings

The updating of the rules in relation to defended family actions introduce an element of judicial case management procedure by means of initial and full case management hearings. From a practitioner's perspective, it probably would be helpful to identify the procedure for the operation of both initial and full Case Management Hearings.

Fixing of date and time for Initial Case Management Hearing – Rule 33.36A

When a Notice of Intention to Defend is lodged, the Sheriff Clerk now requires to fix a date and time for the Initial Case Management Hearing which must be not sooner than 21 days and not later than 49 days after the last date for the lodging of the Notice of Intention to Defend.

Where the case is also involving children where a Section 11 order is being requested, the Sheriff must have regard to holding the Initial Case Management Hearing and the Child Welfare Hearing at the same time.

When the Initial Case Management Hearing is fixed, the Sheriff Clerk has to intimate to the parties in a Form G5A:-

(i) the last date for lodging Defences;

(ii) the date for return of Initial Writ;

(iii) the date of the Initial Case Management Hearing; and

(iv) whether the Child Welfare Hearing is to be held at the same time as the Initial Case Management Hearing.

In terms of Rule 33.36B, as part of the greater judicial case management rules, the Sheriff can alter the date and time for the Initial Case Management Hearing and, in addition, could discharge the hearing. However, on discharging the hearing, there would be an interlocutor issued advising parties that:-

- the hearing has been discharged;
- the last date for lodging Defences;
- the last date for adjustment; and
- a new date and time fixed for an Initial Case Management Hearing.

Sists – Rule 33.36A

Previously in a Sheriff Court action, the action was sisted until such time as either the court recalled the sist or there was a Motion by either party to recall the sist which was granted by the court. Once again, with a view to improving the management of the case, where an action is sisted, the Sheriff Clerk requires:-

- to prepare an interlocutor specifying the reason for the sist;
- fixing a date for a review of the sist hearing not later than 30 days following the expiration of the sist; and
- intimate the date of the review of the sist to each party.

Initial Case Management Hearing – Rule 33.36J

At the initial Case Management Hearing, the Sheriff requires to secure the expeditious progress of the action by ascertaining from parties the matters in dispute and information about the cause.

It is the duty of the parties to provide the Sheriff with sufficient information to enable the Sheriff to conduct the hearing.

Rule 33.36J(3) sets out a detailed list in paragraphs (a) to (p) of the matters on which the parties require to address the court/Sheriff. The factors in relation to child related matters include:-

- whether additional steps require to be taken to give a child an opportunity to express the child's view;
- whether steps require to be taken to investigate any facts or circumstances relating to a child; and

- the suitability of the action for referral to mediation.

At the Initial Case Management Hearing, the Sheriff has to fix a date and time for a full Case Management Hearing on the first suitable court day:-

(a) where there is a crave for a Section 11 order only, not sooner than 16 weeks and not later than 24 weeks after the last date for the lodging of Defences (Rule 33.36F – 14 days after the expiry of the period of notice); and

(b) in all other family actions, not sooner than 20 weeks and not later than 24 weeks after the last date for the lodging of Defences.

Slightly greater priority is given to family actions involving child related matters.

The Sheriff Clerk, following the Initial Case Management Hearing, must intimate to the parties in a Form G6B:-

(a) the last date for lodging a Note of the Basis for any Preliminary Plea;

(b) the last date for adjustment;

(c) the last date for lodging a copy of the Record; and

(d) the date of the full Case Management Hearing.

Pre-Hearing Meeting – Rule 33.36L

In advance of the full Case Management Hearing, the parties (agents) must hold a Pre-Hearing Meeting at which parties must:-

(a) discuss settlement of the action;

(b) agree, so far as possible, the matters which are not in dispute; and

(c) discuss the detailed checklist of factors which are referred to at Rule 33.36P(3).

Not later than two days before the full Case Management hearing, the Pursuer requires to lodge with the court a Joint Minute of the Pre-Hearing Meeting signed by both parties addressing the detailed points in Rule 33.36P(3) or explain to the Sheriff why a Minute has not been lodged.

If either party is not present during the Pre-Hearing Meeting, the parties representative must be able to contact the party during the meeting and be in full possession of all relevant facts.

All parties must except on cause shown attend personally both the Initial Case Management Hearing and full Case Management Hearing.

Adjustment of pleadings – Rule 33.36M

(a) Parties may adjust their pleadings until 14 days before the date of the full Case Management Hearing or any continuation of that hearing;

(b) any adjustments must be exchanged between parties and not lodged in process;

(c) parties are responsible for maintaining a record of adjustments made during the period of adjustment; and

(d) no adjustments are permitted after that period except with leave of court.

Record for Full Case Management Hearing – Rule 33.36N

At the end of the period of adjustment, and prior to the full Case Management Hearing, the Purser in the action requires to prepare a Record, a certified copy of which requires to be lodged not later than two days before the Full Case Management Hearing.

In the event of the Full Case Management Hearing being continued and there being further adjustment or amendment then a copy of the Record as adjusted or amended requires to be lodged with the court not later than two days before the Full Case Management Hearing.

Exchange of Lists of Witnesses – Rule 33.36O

Not later than seven days prior to the Full Case Management Hearing, each party must:-

(a) intimate to the other party a List of Witnesses, including any skilled witnesses on whose evidence they intend to rely at Proof; and

(b) lodge a copy of that list in process.

The List of Witnesses must include:-

(a) the name, occupation (where known) and address of each witness;

(b) a summary of up to fifty words on the matters to which each witness is expected to seek; and

(c) details of whether the witness is considered to be a vulnerable witness and whether any child witness notice or vulnerable witness application has been lodged in respect of that witness in terms of the Vulnerable Witnesses (Scotland) Act 2004.

Full Case Management Hearing – Rule 33.36P

Just as with the Initial Case Management Hearing, at the Full Case Management Hearing, the Sheriff requires to seek to secure the expeditious progress of the action by ascertaining from the parties the matters in dispute and information about any other matters referred to in terms of that particular Rule.

Once again, there is a duty on the parties to provide the Sheriff with sufficient information to enable the Sheriff to conduct the hearing.

At the Full Case Management Hearing, each party must address the court on a detailed checklist of factors which are set out in paragraphs (a) to (p) of Rule 33.36P(3) which in relation to child matters include:-

- whether additional steps require to be taken to give a child an opportunity to express the child's view;
- whether steps require to be taken to investigate any facts or circumstances relating to a child;
- the suitability of the action for referral to mediation; and
- whether special measures will required for the purposes of taking the evidence of any vulnerable witnesses.

At the Full Case Management Hearing, the Sheriff requires to:-

(a) close the Record and fix a Pre-Proof Hearing in accordance with Rule 28A (Pre-Proof Hearing);

(b) appoint the action to a Proof and make such orders as to the extent of the Proof, the lodging of a Joint Minute of Admissions or agreement or such other matters as the Sheriff thinks fit;

(c) deal with any Notice lodged until Rule 22.1 (Note of Basis of Preliminary Plea);

(d) appoint the cause to a Proof before Answer; or

(e) in considering any Rule 22.1 (Note), appoint matters to a Debate.

It is thought that it is unlikely that there will be Preliminary Pleas which will require a Proof before Answer or a Debate where there is a family action involving Section 11 orders. The issue would arise where there are both financial and Section 11 orders and essentially, where the preliminary pleas in relation to the financial matters merit or require a Debate. That of itself could delay not only the conclusion of financial issues but also delay the final determination of child care issues in relation to Section 11.

Once again, to ensure the expeditious progress of case, when a Diet of Proof is being fixed, it will be assigned for the appropriate number of days for resolution of the issues. In addition, the Sheriff can make such orders as are fit to ensure the expeditious resolution of the issues in dispute, including:

(a) restricting the issues for Proof;

(b) the scope for instruction of a joint expert or a meeting between skilled persons;

(c) excluding specified documents, reports or witnesses from Proof;

(d) fixing other hearings; and

(e) awarding expenses.

Judicial continuity – Rule 33.36Q

The same Sheriff (where possible) is to preside at:-

(a) the Initial Case Management Hearing;

(b) the full Case Management Hearing;

(c) the Pre-Proof Hearing;

(d) where fixed, any

  (i) Child Welfare Hearing;

  (ii) Proof;

  (iii) Proof before Answer;

  (iv) Debate.

These rules are relatively new. We are presently at the stage where Initial and Full Case Management Hearings are being fixed in actions covered by the amended Rules introduced in September 2023. Whilst it is the early stages of the operation of the new Rules, it is clear that the Rules set out and represent a significant change to the management of family and child care issues in the Sheriff Court. On the basis that the rules are properly adhered to, it is likely that they will prevent undue delay in proceedings relating to the welfare of the children, and will enable significant greater judicial case management to ensure family cases are resolved more quickly.

CHAPTER SIX

APPLICATIONS UNDER THE CHILD ABDUCTION & CUSTODY ACT 1985 – THE 1980 HAGUE CONVENTION

The 1980 Hague Convention on Civil Aspects of International Child Abduction

The premise behind the 1980 Hague Convention is that it is in the best interests of children to be returned to their country of habitual residence and for the courts there to make decisions about their welfare (for example, which parent they should live with).

The 1980 Convention is one of the most widely endorsed international treaties we have, with over 100 signatories.

Domestic legislation

The 1980 Hague Convention was brought into force in the UK by *The Child Abduction and Custody Act 1985* (CACA 1985). In Scotland the Court of Session is the only court with jurisdiction to hear cases under the 1980 Hague Convention (*section 4, CACA 1985*).

The *Child Abduction Act 1984* (CAA 1984) is the domestic legislation that creates the criminal offence of child abduction. The CAA 1984 is divided into different sections for Scotland and for England and Wales. One significant difference is that the criminal offence of child abduction is only committed under the law of Scotland where a person connected with a child under 16 takes or keeps a child out of the UK **in breach of a UK court order** dealing with the custody of the child or prohibiting a child's removal from the UK (unless they have appropriate consent) (*section 6(1), CAA 1984*). This is more restrictive than the English offence which can be committed if the child's removal is without the consent of persons with parental responsibility, regardless of whether any court order is in place (*section 1(3), CAA 1984*).

The 1980 Hague Convention

The Convention is defined in Section 1(1) of the CACA 1985 and Schedule 1 in the Act. The Convention is split into 6 Chapters and the relevant provisions are as follows:-

- Chapter 1 – Scope of Convention

  This sets out when the removal or retention of a child is wrongful (Article 3). It applies in respect of any child who was *habitually resident* in a Contracting State immediately before any breach of custody or access rights (Article 4). It also defines rights of custody and access (Article 5).

- Chapter 2 – Central Authorities

  This deals with the role and the powers of the central authorities. In Scotland the Scottish Central Authority was set up by the Justice Directorate of the Scottish Government and has, among other duties, responsibility for incoming applications (where a child has been abducted to Scotland) and outgoing applications (where a child has been abducted from Scotland). In Particular Article 7 sets out an obligation on Central Authorities to co-operate with each other to achieve the objects of the Convention.

- Chapter 3 – Return of Children

  This sets out:

  - the information needed to submit a return application via the central authorities (Article 8);
  - that return proceedings should be dealt with expeditiously and within six weeks (Article 11);
  - that there is a settlement defence should the return proceedings commence after the child has been wrongfully removed or wrongfully retained for more than one year (Article 12);
  - each defence to the return order (Article 13 covered in more detail below); and
  - that any decision taken under the 1980 Hague Convention is not a determination on the merits of custody (Article 19). This reinforces the purpose of the 1980 Hague Convention; a summary procedure to return children who have been abducted to their country of habitual residence so that country can make decisions regarding their welfare.

- Chapter 4 – Rights of Access

  Article 21 provides that an application to secure the effective exercise of rights of access can be made through a central authority, in the same way as an application for return of a child.

- Chapter 5 – General Provisions

  This deals with miscellaneous provisions, including the availability of legal aid for applications (Article 25). The availability of legal aid varies from country to country. In Scotland, non-means-tested legal aid is available to petitioners and means-tested legal aid is available to respondents.

- Chapter 6 – Final Clauses

  This deals with final clauses and ratification.

The test

In order to successfully raise a Petition under the 1980 Hague Convention, applicants require to show: –

1. The children are under 16
2. The children were habitually resident in the jurisdiction prior to the wrongful retention or removal
3. The wrongful retention or removal is in breach of the applicant's custody right; and that
4. The applicant was exercising their rights of custody prior to the wrongful retention.

Habitual residence

There is no definition of habitual residence in the 1980 Hague Convention, but it is generally considered to be the place where a child is integrated in a social and family environment.

Habitual residence is a matter of fact that has to be considered on a case-by-case basis. This can be demonstrated by a variety of factors which may include:

- The language the child speaks;
- Where they go to school;
- Where they are registered with doctors and dentists;
- Where the child's family and friends are based.

In the case of A v A [2013] UKSC 60, which was a Supreme Court UK case, Baroness Hale of Richmond examined habitual residence and she drew together the threads of the previous case law and provided critical relevant points for consideration. The various threads were:-

- Habitual residence is a question of fact and not a legal concept such as domicile. There is no legal rule akin to that whereby a child automatically takes the domicile of his or her parents.
- The purpose of the Child Abduction & Custody Act 1985 was to adopt a concept which was the same as that adopted in the Hague and European Conventions.
- The test adopted by the European Court is "The place which reflects some degree of integration by the child in a social and family environment" in the country concerned. This depends upon numerous factors, including the reasons for the family stay at the country in question.
- The social and family environment of an infant or young child is shared with those (whether parents or others) upon whom he or she is dependent. Hence it is necessary to assess the integration of that person or persons in the social and family environment of the country concerned.
- The essential factual and individual nature of the enquiry should not be glossed with legal concepts which would produce a

different result from that which the factual enquiry would produce.

- It is possible that a child may have no country of habitual residence at a particular point in time, although that would be in the exceptional cases.

It was noted by Baroness Hale that in certain circumstances, a child could acquire a new habitual residence in a single day dependent upon circumstances.

There are two other cases that are of significant relevance here, one of which is a case called In re R [2015] UKSC 35 where Lord Reed, in a Scottish case heard by the UK Supreme Court, emphasised that it was the stability of the residence of the child that was important and not whether that residence was of a permanent character. Lord Reed observed in that particular case:-

"Following the childrens' move with their mother to Scotland, that was where they lived, albeit for what was intended to be a period of twelve months. Their life there had the necessary quality of stability. For the time being, their home was in Scotland. Their social life was there. Their family life was predominantly there. The longer time went on, the more deeply integrated they had become into their environment in Scotland. The court considered the evidence on a proper understanding on the nature of habitual resident. In light of the evidence before the court, their conclusion was that the children were habitually resident in Scotland at the material time."

There was, in fact, no requirement that the child should have been resident in a country for a particular time, let alone there should be the intention of a party to reside there permanently or indefinitely and accordingly we see the move away from the intentions of the parties and the focus upon the circumstances of the child in any particular environment.

Finally, there is a decision of Lady Wise in The Outer House of the Court of Session in 2021, in the case of F -v- M 2021 CSOH 90. This is an important decision because it instructs us that parents are not able to contract out of the Convention. It was noted that the children had shared a home with both parents in Scotland, had attended school, visited extended family and socialised with friends and Lady Wise found that, as a matter of fact, their habitual residence had altered.

The parents in this case had entered into an agreement in New Zealand which was designed as "legally binding" and provided *inter alia* that the children were born in New Zealand, New Zealand was the place of habitual residence for the children. "The period of time that the children remained in the United Kingdom during the trial period shall not affect their place of residence; Further that neither party should have the ability to retain the children in the UK without the consent of the other parent."

Lady Wise formed the view that whilst the intentions of the parties in June 2020 were to come to Scotland only for a trial period without it altering the children's habitual residence, as a matter of fact that habitual residence had changed by 3rd June when the (mother) initiated divorce proceedings and sought and obtained orders the following day in relation to the children including an interim interdict against their removal from the UK. Lady Wise indicated that formal agreements entered into in good faith by two adults of sound mind should not be readily ignored or set aside. Whilst the unusual feature of the case is the detail of the agreement and its formality, the principle remains the same. It accords with the policy of the convention that children are not parcels or property whose future can be determined solely by the contracts or actions of adults. If in an agreement, a child's habitual residence will not change that cannot be enforced if, as a matter of fact, that child's residence is found to have changed. The development of the law on habitual residence as it applies to Hague Convention cases appears, as Lady Wise observed, to have resulted in parents now being effectively unable to enter into a directly enforceable agreement on the temporary relocation of their children. Such agreements remain relevant as a factor, but will not be adhered to where the necessary social and family integration of the children in the "new" country is shown to be of a well settled character. Whilst it may be that different views exist in other Hague Convention jurisdictions about the relative significance of a formal agreement entered into with the benefit of legal advice, in Scotland, it is clear that no matter how formal the agreement, the analysis of the circumstance of the children at the material time must be the primary focus of the discussion. Each case is sufficiently fact sensitive that no absolute rules have been laid down. Had the children been less settled in Scotland, it may be that the nature and terms of the agreement would have had greater weight. However, on the current understanding of habitual residence as it applies to the Hague Convention, the agreement could never have been determinative.

Defences

When a child is brought to Scotland in a potential international child abduction situation, and the parent in the original country seeks their return, proceedings are raised in the Court of Session by solicitors instructed by the Scottish Central Authority. The parent in Scotland can then instruct solicitors to try to advance one of the limited defences on their behalf in terms of Article 13 of the Convention, if appropriate.

These potential defences are:

1. The applicant with care of the child was not actually exercising the custody rights at the time of removal or retention;

2. consent/ acquiescence;

3. objection of the child to return;

4. grave risk that return would expose the child to physical or psychological harm or place them in an intolerable situation(Article 13(b)); or

5. settlement i.e that the child is now settled in their new environment (which may only be engaged if the child has been living there for 12 months or more) .

Chapter 70 of the Rules of Court of the Court of Session

These Rules of Court set out that an application for the return of a child, for organising or protecting rights of access granted by any court of a contracting party to the Hague Convention or an application under Section 8 for declarator that removal or retention was wrongful is to be made by Petition and it sets out the averments which are to be included in the relevant Petition which includes:-

(i) The identity of the Petitioner and the person alleged to have removed or retained the child;

(ii) The identity of the child and date of birth;

(iii) The whereabouts or suspected whereabouts of the child, the date in which the child is alleged to have been wrongfully removed;

(iv) The grounds on which the Petition is based/the proceedings which gave custody to the Petitioner, any civil cause and dependence before any other court or authority in respect of the child for the proceedings under the Hague Convention in relation to which the Petition is necessary;

(v) There is a requirement to produce with the Petition a certificate copy/authorised copy of any relevant decision or agreement; and

(vi) Evidence by Affidavits of any witnesses and any documentary evidence, whether originals or copies in support of the Petition. The Rules also set out the period of notice for lodging Answers to a Petition, which will be four days, and the date for the first order hearing which will be a date within seven days after expiry of the period of notice for a first hearing to determine the progress of the Petition.

The Rules also deal with warrant and forms for intimation to a child and for seeking a child's views as set out in Rules 70.6(5), 70.16 and 70.17.

Summary

Therefore, if a child has been abducted to Scotland from another Hague Convention country then the parent in that country – the left behind parent – would make an application through the central authority for the return of their child, who will appoint a solicitor to them from their list.

Equally, if the child has been taken from Scotland to another country, then the parent here would make an application through the two central authorities, and the case would be heard in that other country. How the outcome will be determined will be very much on a fact sensitive basis.

CHAPTER SEVEN

THE CHILDREN (SCOTLAND) ACT 2020

The Children (Scotland) Act 2020 received Royal Assent on 1st October 2020. The substantive provisions of the Act are not yet in force. This is to provide the Government, local authorities, the courts, children's hearings and other bodies time to prepare for the substantial changes which the Act brings prior to the organisations and agencies having to deliver them. The new Act covers a number of issues but the main thrust of the Act is:-

(i) to bring Scots Law into line with children's rights under the United Nations Convention on the Rights of the Child (UNCRC) to ensure that children's views are heard in family court cases, children's hearings and adoptions hearings and that the best interests of children are at the front and centre of these cases; and

(ii) provides additional protection to victims of domestic abuse, including children.

The first part of the Act is very much focused on giving additional prominence to the views of the children, whether in court hearings or children's hearings. The main elements can be summarised as:-

(i) Children and young people will have more opportunity to give their views to the court and children's hearings in a way they choose;

(ii) Support is provided to keep children in contact with their brothers and sisters, whether in court proceedings or in a Children's Hearing;

(iii) Additional protection for vulnerable witnesses and parties in court;

(iv) The investigation by the court of reasons for Section 11 orders not being complied with; and

(v) Avoidance of delay in proceedings involving children which effectively represents a restatement or an enshrinement in the law of the opinion of Supreme Court in NJDB -v- JEG 2012 UKSC 21.

The second part of the Act deals with additional services that will be set up as a consequence of the Act which includes:-

(i) advocacy Workers in family court cases;

(ii) a new register of Child Welfare Reporters and Curators ad litem;

(iii) a register of Solicitors appointed where a person has been prohibited from personally conducting a case themselves in relation to vulnerable witnesses where the court is considering making an order under Section 11 of the Children (Scotland) Act 1995 and children's hearings;

(iv) alternatives to court, the funding of alternative dispute resolution; and

(v) the regulation of contact centres.

This chapter deals with the substantive provisions rather than the additional services that will be introduced by the Act.

Children and Young People

With the introduction of the Act, children will have more opportunity to give their views to the court.

With that in mind, it would be helpful to consider:-

(i) the present legal provisions in relation to children's views as set out in the Children (Scotland) Act 1995;

(ii) set out what the landscape will be once the 2020 Act provisions come into force;

(iii) comment on the changes that this will bring; and

(iv) consider current judicial thinking.

The current Law

This is set out in Section 11(7) of the Children (Scotland) Act 1995.

Subsection (7) sets out that, subject to subsection (8), in considering whether or not to make an order under subsection (1) (which is an order in relation to a child whether it be in relation to contact, residence or specific issue order) the court –

(a) shall regard the welfare of the child concerned as its paramount consideration and shall not make any such order unless it considers that it would be better for the child that the order be made than that none should be made at all; and

(b) taking account of the child's age and maturity, shall so far as practicable –

(i) give him an opportunity to indicate whether he wishes to express his views;

(ii) if he does so wish, give him an opportunity to express them; and

(iii) have regard to such views as he may express.

In terms of subsection (7)(A) in carrying out the duties imposed by subsection 7(a), the court shall have regard, in particular, to the matters mentioned in subsection (7B).

Those matters are:-

(a) the need to protect the child from –

(i) any abuse; or

(ii) the risk of any abuse,

which affects, or might affect, the child.

(b) the effect such abuse, or the risk of such abuse, might have on the child;

(c) the ability of a person –

(i) who has carried out abuse which affects or might affect the child; or

(ii) who might carry out such abuse,

to care for, or otherwise meet the needs of, the child; and

(d) the effect any abuse, or the risk of any abuse, might have on the carrying out of responsibilities in connection with the welfare of the child by a person who has (or, by virtue or an order under subsection (i) would have) those responsibilities.

(7C)

In subsection (7B) above –

"abuse" includes –

(a) violence, harassment, threatening conduct and any other conduct giving rise, or likely to give rise, to physical or mental injury, fear, alarm or distress;

(b) abuse of a person other than the child; and

(c) domestic abuse

"conduct" includes –

(a) speech; and

(b) presence in a specified place or area.

(7D)

Where –

(a) the court is considering making an order under subsection (i) above; and

(b) in pursuance of the order, two or more relevant persons would have to cooperate with one another as respects matters affecting the child,

the court, shall consider whether it is appropriate to make the order.

(7E)

In subsection (7D) above, "relevant person", in relation to a child means –

(a) a person having parental responsibilities or parental rights in respect of the child; or

(b) where a parent of the child does not have parental responsibilities or parental rights in respect of the child, a parent of the child.

In terms of Subsection 10, without prejudice to the generality of paragraph (b) of subsection (7) above, a child twelve years of age or more shall be presumed to be of sufficient age and maturity to form a view for the purposes both of that paragraph and of subsection (9) above.

Law after Children (Scotland) Act 2020 comes into force

Subsections (7) to (7E) and (9) and (10) in terms of the 1995 Act are being repealed and are to be replaced with:-

Section 11ZA – Paramountcy of child's welfare, and the non-intervention presumption.

"(1). In deciding whether or not to make an order under Section 11(1) and what order (if any) to make, the court must regard the welfare of the child concerned as its paramount consideration."

(2). "The court must not make an order under Section 11(1) unless it considers it would be better for the child concerned that the order be made than that none should be made at all."

(2A) When considering the child's welfare, the court is to have regard to any risk of prejudice to the child's welfare that delay in proceedings would pose."

(3). "When considering the child's welfare and whether it would be better for the child to make an order than not, the court must have regard to the following matters in particular:-

(a) the need to protect the child from abuse, or the risk of abuse, which affects or might affect the child,

(b) the effect that abuse, or the risk of abuse might have on the child,

(c) the ability of a person to care for, or otherwise meet the needs of, the children, where that person has carried out or might carry out abuse, which affects, or might affect, the child,

(d) the effect that abuse, or the risk of abuse, might have on the carrying out of responsibilities in connection with the welfare of the children by a person who has (or, by virtue of an order under Section 11(1) would have) those responsibilities,

(e) whether it is, or would be, appropriate for an order to require that two or more persons cooperate with one another with regard to matters affecting the child,

(f) the effect that the order the court is deciding whether or not to make might have on:-

(i) the involvement of the child's parents in bringing the child up; and

(ii) the child's important relationships with other people."

(4). "abuse" includes –

(a) violence, harassment, threatening conduct and any other conduct giving rise; or likely to give rise, to physical or mental injury, fear, alarm or distress;

(b) abuse of a person other than the child; and

(c) domestic abuse."

"conduct" includes –

(a) speech, and

(b) presence in a particular place or area.

11(ZB) – Regard to be had to the child's views

(1) In deciding whether or not to make an order under Section 11(1) and what order (if any) to make, the court must –

(a) give the child concerned an opportunity to express the child's views in:-

(i) the manner that the child prefers; or

(ii) a manner that is suitable to the child if the child has not indicated a preference or it would not be reasonable in the circumstances to accommodate the child's preference; and

(b) have regard to any views expressed by the child, taking into account the child's age and maturity.

(2) But the court is not required to comply with subsection (1) if satisfied that –

(a) the child is not capable of forming a view; or

(b) the location of the child is not known.

(3) The child is presumed to be capable of forming a view unless the contrary is shown.

(4) Nothing in this section requires a child to be legally represented in any proceedings in which the child's views are sought, if the child does not wish to be.

I discuss the issue of delay later. However, it appears that the paramountcy and non-intervention provisions of the present Act are essentially re-enacted.

Section 11(ZA) sets out a list of specific factors for the court to consider in deciding what order (if any) to make. We do not have the checklists which appear in Section 1(3)(a) – (g) of the Children Act 1989 in England and Wales which requires the court to consider a list of specific factors such as the child's physical, emotional and educational needs, age, sex and background, his or her wishes and the capacity of a parent to meet those needs.

The factors set out in Section 11(ZA)(3) require a consideration of the impact the court's order might be expected to have on the parents and children involved in the case, including siblings who would include "the child's important relationships with other people" Section 11(ZA)(3)(f). Accordingly, there is once enacted a greater emphasis and weight to be attached to the impact the order would have on the child.

Section 11 E Duty to consider child's best interests when allowing access to information

(1) Where the court—

(a) is considering making an order under section 11(1), and

(b) has to decide whether a person should have access to anything in which private information about a child is recorded, in making that decision it must comply with subsections (2) and (3) in relation to that child.

(2) The court must regard the best interests of the child as its primary consideration.

(3) The court must—

(a) give the child an opportunity to express the child's views in—

(i) the manner that the child prefers, or

(ii) a manner that is suitable to the child if the child has not indicated a preference or it would not be reasonable in the circumstances to accommodate the child's preference, and

(b) have regard to any views expressed by the child, taking into account the child's age and maturity.

(4) But the court is not required to comply with subsection (3) if satisfied that—

(a) the child is not capable of forming a view, or

(b) the location of the child is not known.

(5) The child is to be presumed to be capable of forming a view unless the contrary is shown.

(6) "private information" means information in which the child could have a reasonable expectation of privacy.

11(F) – Explanation of court decisions to the child

(1) This section applies when –

(a) the court decides whether or not to make an order under Section 11(1);

(b) the court decides to vary or discharge an order made under Section 11(1); and

(c) the court –

(i) decides to decline to vary or discharge an order made under Section 11(1), and

(ii) considers it appropriate to explain that decision to the child concerned

(2) The court must ensure the decision is explained to the child concerned in a way the child can understand.

(3) The court is not required to comply with subsection (2), if satisfied that -

(a) the child would not be capable of understanding an explanation however given,

(b) it is not in the best interests of the child to give an explanation; or

(c) the location of the child is not known.

(4) The court may fulfil its duty under subsection (2) by

(a) giving the explanation to the child itself; or

(b) arranging for it to be given by a Child Welfare Reporter.

A decision includes an interim decision (11)(F)(5).

Whilst this sets out the law which will apply once the Act comes into force, there appears to be three main factors in which there is a significant change from the present legal position.

- Children require to be afforded the opportunity of expressing their views in their preferred manner;

- Children are presumed to be capable of forming a view, regardless of age; and

- There is a requirement to explain the decisions of the court to children.

The present Section 11(7)(b)(i) – (iii) provides that:-

- children must be given an opportunity to indicate if they wish to express a view and, if so, the opportunity to express a view;

- the court has to have regard to such views taking account of the child's age and maturity;

- a child aged twelve years of age or more is presumed to be of sufficient age and maturity to form a view (Section 11(10)).

The new Section 11(ZB)(1)(a) provides that in deciding whether or not to make an order, the court must give the child an opportunity to express a view;-

(i) in the manner that the child prefers; or

(ii) a manner that is suitable to the child if the child has not indicated a preference or it would not be reasonable in the circumstances to accommodate the child's preference.

Similar provisions apply in both adoption and children's hearings.

The new Act represents a different and significant approach from the present legal position. Subject to very limited exceptions, the court must now enable the view of a child to be taken and in a manner that the child wishes. The whole thrust of the Act is to make the court process for children expressing a view less intimidating and more accessible. Once it is in force, the court will require to:-

1. firstly, give a child an opportunity to express a view as opposed to give the child an opportunity to indicate whether the child wishes to express a view; and

2. secondly, if so, identify how the child would like to do that, failing which, it requires to do so in a manner that is suitable (appropriate) for the child.

A range of options appropriate to the child's age will require to be offered in order to facilitate how a child should express their view.

The child may wish to speak to the Sheriff, complete a Form F9 (as at present) at home, complete a Form F9 with the assistance of a Teacher, Youth Worker, express a view via drawings, notes, videos, visuals or play therapy. Section 21 of the 2020 Act places a duty on Scottish Ministers to ensure availability of child advocacy services for children and in family court cases. Accordingly, the views of the child could be obtained/communicated through a child advocacy worker.

Once the view of the child has been obtained or communicated then the court's role remains as at present, to have regard to any views expressed by a child taking into account the child's age and maturity (Section 11(ZB)(1)(b)). The court does not need to comply with that duty if satisfied that:-

(a) the child is not capable of forming a view; or

(b) the location of the child is not known.

With the new Act, a child of any age is presumed to be capable of forming a view. The present presumption regarding a child of twelve or more being presumed to form or being able to form a view is replaced and will be repealed and substituted with "the child is to be presumed to be capable of forming a view unless the contrary is shown" – Section 11(ZB)(3).

Explaining decisions of the court

Section 11(F) inserted by Section 20 provides that an explanation must be given when the court decides whether or not to make an order under Section 11(1) – residence or contact. An explanation always needs to be given when the court decides to vary or discharge an order. This includes interim orders.

If the court decides to decline to vary or discharge an order, an explanation only has to be given to the child if the court considers it is appropriate to explain that decision to the child concerned.

The explanation requires to be conveyed or given in a way that the child can understand. The court is only excused from that obligation to provide an explanation on being satisfied that:-

(a) the child would not be capable of understanding an explanation, however given;

(b) it is not in the best interests of the child to give an explanation; or

(c) the location of the child is not known.

If a child's views are not sought initially, then that may be the basis for setting out that the child would not be capable of understanding the explanation. Communicating a decision which is not in the best interests of the child is more problematic. Whilst there may be sensitive details about the adults' relationship, the view may be taken that an explanation could still be provided as that would be in a way that the child could understand. In M -v- C 2021 CISH 14, this related to a Sheriff's decision not to seek the view of a child just under five as the Sheriff had concerns about communicating to the child information of which the child should not be told, the court indicated that such matters could be guarded against. There is the option in terms of Section 11F(4) given to the Sheriff or Judge for the court to either give the explanation itself or arrange for it to be given by a Child Welfare Reporter.

On the basis that the child's views are sought prior to any decision being made regarding any order, then the way that the child's views are initially sought may well be the basis for communicating the decision. There is also the issue in a Child Welfare Hearing where the Sheriff makes a decision immediately if the child is not there then the decision is likely to be communicated to the child by either one or both parents. There is therefore perhaps a requirement for the decision to be communicated immediately to the child.

In summary, it is clear that the way children's views are to be obtained (when the Act becomes law), from the present methods of a Sheriff speaking to a child or via a Form F9, will significantly change. There requires to be significant training and development of support services, updating of the court rules (which has now occurred since 23 September 2023) and the court process. The number of children whose views are to be sought will significantly increase; the age and maturity of the children whose views are being sought will be significantly younger in age and of lesser maturity but greater in number than is at present taking account of the presumption of all children being capable of forming a view and decisions having to be communicated to children with some minor exceptions. Taking the views of younger children, four/five years old, will take greater care than from say a ten/eleven year-old. Whilst the main legislative provisions of the Act are not yet in force, and an indication has not yet been provided by the Scottish Government as to when those provisions are to be in force, it is obvious that significant resources for training and implementation of the provisions of the Act are required. It would appear that the task to allow the main provisions to be implemented places a significantly greater onus on family lawyers in child disputes. What however is clear is that the circumstances which arose in LRK -v- AG 2021 SAC CIV 1, where a Sheriff did not seek the views of a six/seven year-old child, is highly unlikely to occur even prior to the 2020 Act coming into force.

Duty to investigate failure to obey orders under Section 11

If an order for contact or residence has not been complied with, an individual seeking to enforce the order may seek to hold the person not complying with the court order to be in contempt of court.

In terms of Section 15(2) of the Contempt of Court Act 1981 where the contempt is dealt with by the Sheriff in connection with civil proceedings, the penalty for contempt is a maximum of three months' imprisonment or a fine of level four on the standard scale, currently £2,500, or both.

The standard of proof in contempt proceedings which are sui generis is beyond reasonable doubt. Imprisonment ordered is civil imprisonment and the contempt proceedings are not criminal. However, it is for the individual who is not obtaining the benefit of the Section 11 order to pursue the action for contempt by way of a Minute for Contempt procedure. These are proceedings which are separate from the contact or residence dispute. Contempt proceedings, in practice, can be both time consuming and an expensive process but ought not to be. A number of opportunities may be provided to the person not complying with the court order to comply with it prior to the court making a determination.

Section 22 of the 2020 Act inserts a new Section 11G and sets out:-

(1)

(a) where a court is considering whether to find a person in contempt for failing to obey an order under Section 11; or

(b) vary or discharge an order under Section 11 on the basis that a person has failed to obey it then the court

(2) if satisfied that the person has failed to obey the order, the court must:-

(a) seek to establish the reasons for the failure; and

(b) in so doing,

(i) give the child an opportunity to express a view in

(A) the manner that the child prefers; or

(B) in a manner that is suitable to the child if the child has not indicated a preference or it would not be reasonable in the circumstances to accommodate the child's preference and

(ii) have regard to any views expressed by the child taking into account the child's age and maturity.

The court has the option of appointing a child welfare reporter to investigate and report to the court on the person's failure or alleged failure – Section 11G(5).

Whilst the provisions are not yet in force, but whilst the court has a duty to investigate, it can only do so if the court is satisfied that the person has failed to obey the order – Section 11G(2). If the person disputes that he/she has failed to obey the order then, presumably, a hearing will require to take place and, only within the confines of that hearing, obtain the child's views.

It would be interesting to see how the court applies the provisions of that subsection once it is in force. This has to be compared with the Minute for Contempt proceedings. In such contempt proceedings, the court, in a refusal to facilitate contact requires to establish:-

(i) the court made an order for contact;

(ii) contact did not take place; and

(iii) failure resulted from disobedience.

This is set out in terms of the case of CM -v- SM 2017 SC 23. By contrast, the issue in a contact action will be different as it will focus on what is best for the child. The views of the child do not require to be taken in a Minute for Contempt procedure whereas the views of the child will require to be taken in a Section 11G procedure once in force.

Delay in proceedings likely to prejudice a child's welfare

In terms of the new Section 11 of the Children (Scotland) Act, the court and children's hearing have to have regard to the risk of prejudice to the child's welfare that delay in proceedings would hold.

The Supreme Court, in 2012, set out in NJDB -v- JEG 2012 UKSC 21 that delay in the progression of proceedings in relation to children may determine the issue and, accordingly, delay requires to be avoided. The avoidance of delay is an aspect of current good practice, taking account of the Supreme Court decision. Whilst it could be argued it is part of the law of Scotland at the present time, including this in an Act of Parliament emphasises the importance of avoiding delay and places a clear legal obligation on courts, lawyers and parties to avoid delay wherever possible.

It could be argued that as a consequence of the binding decision of the Supreme Court decision NJDB -v- JEG and the case management provisions which have been introduced into the Rules of Court, both in the Sheriff Court (since September of last year) and the Court of Session, that Section 11(G) is possibly unnecessary. In addition, in relation to the investigation of failures to comply with a court order, this only applies if there a finding of contempt or failure to comply after an evidential hearing.

Support to keep children in contact with brothers and sisters/siblings

Sections 13 and 14 of the 2020 Act arose as a consequence of what was the uncovering of a "gap" in the Children's Hearing system which has had to be adapted to meet the requirements of Article 8 in relation to siblings and other family members as set out in ABC v Principal Reporter and Another 2020 UKSC 26. In that case, whilst the court decided that public authorities did not require to give a sibling the status of a relevant person, there was a clear recognition of the interest of both the child and the sibling in maintaining a sibling relationship through contact or through placement in most cases. The Supreme Court indicated there required to be bespoke enquiry about the child's relationship with his or her siblings when the children's hearing is addressing the possibility of a Compulsory Supervision Order (CSO).

Section 13 of the 2020 Act amended Section 17 of the 1995 Act to provide that the local authority must take such steps to promote personal relationships and direct contact between a looked after child and their siblings, having regard to the local authority's duty to promote the welfare of the child.

The section also amended Section 17(3) to the effect that before making any decision with respect to a child they are looking after, or are proposing to look after, a local authority shall, so far as reasonably practicable, ascertain the views of siblings and any other person with whom the child has lived and with whom the child has an ongoing relationship, and the character of a relationship between the siblings.

In addition, Section 14 of the Act revised Section 29(a) of the Children's Hearing (Scotland) Act 2011 placing a requirement on the decision maker, when deciding whether to include a direction regulating contact between the child and a relevant person in relation to the child, a sibling or the child or any other person with whom the child has resided and with whom the child has an ongoing relationship with the character of a sibling relationship, the decision maker must consider relationships between the child and their siblings and between the child and the relevant persons. Following upon the Act receiving royal assent, Sections 13 and 14 came into force on 26th July 2022.

Taking together the new provisions means sibling relationships will have to be prioritised when decisions are taken about children and young people in every day social work practice. Children's hearings practice should become more consistent and siblings will be able to know their rights and what to expect.

It should also be noted that the opportunity to participate in a children's hearing and to appeal against a relevant person decision, being children's hearings provisions, in terms of Sections 25 and 26 also came into force on 26th July 2022 on the basis that these were related to and flowed naturally from the provisions of Section 13 and 14 so children's views will be afforded greater weight.

Vulnerable witnesses and parties in civil proceedings

Sections 4 to 7 of the Act introduced new special measures to be used to assist vulnerable witnesses and parties in civil proceedings arising out of children's hearings or when the court is considering making an order under Section 11 of the 1995 Act.

In court proceedings where a Section 11(1) order may be made, a person will be deemed to be a vulnerable witness if they are protected by a civil protection order from conduct or where the person is a victim or complainer in respect of certain criminal offences committed or alleged to have been committed by a party to the proceedings. The Act introduces special measures where the court may authorise for the purpose of taking the evidence of a vulnerable witness. Those special measures permit the court to prohibit parties to the proceedings from personally conducting their own case where there is either abuse or alleged abuse. Such a person who is subject to a prohibition will be given an opportunity to appoint their own Solicitor. If they decline to do so, the court will appoint one from a Register of Solicitors which is to be set up in terms of Section 7 of the Act.

CHAPTER EIGHT

SERVICES TO BE INTRODUCED AND UPDATED BY THE CHILDREN (SCOTLAND) ACT 2020

In this chapter, it is proposed to look at new services which are to be introduced by the 2020 Act or an enhancement/evolvement of services which can assist both the courts and children's hearings in the resolution of child centred disputes.

Advocacy Services

Section 21 of the Act imposes a duty on Scottish Ministers to make such provision as they consider necessary and sufficient to ensure that all children concerned in relevant proceedings have access to appropriate child advocacy services.

Child advocacy services are defined as "services of support and representation for the purposes of assisting a child in relation to the child's involvement in relevant proceedings" and "relevant proceedings" means proceedings in which the court is considering making an order under Section 11(1).

This could include, once advocacy services are available, a means of obtaining the views of children and communicating those views to the Sheriff "in a manner that the child prefers or a manner that is suitable to the child if the child has not indicated a preference" – Section 11(ZB). Whilst it would ordinarily have been assumed or thought that a child advocacy worker could perhaps communicate a court's decision to the child which requires to be given, this appears to be excluded by the provisions of Section 11F(4) as the explanation can only be given by the court itself or by either a Child Welfare Reporter.

Child Welfare Reporters, Curators ad litem and Section 7 Solicitors

The Act, in Section 7, requires the establishment of a Register of Solicitors who can be appointed where a person is prohibited from personally conducting their case. Section 9 requires the establishment of a Register of Child Welfare Reporters and Section 17 requires the establishment of a Register of Curators ad litem.

The current practice of appointing Child Welfare Reporters and curators ad litem is dealt with on a Sheriffdom by Sheriffdom basis. Child Welfare Reporters are also appointed in the Court of Session as are Curators ad Litem. As indicated, the 2020 Act introduced a special measure into the Vulnerable Witnesses (Scotland) 2004 prohibiting a party from personally conducting their case in certain circumstances where a Section 11 order may be made.

However, in order to protect the right to a fair trial, an individual who has been prohibited from conducting their case has to be provided with legal representation. The Act gives Scottish Ministers the power to establish a Register of Solicitors from whom a Solicitor is to be appointed if a party so prohibited fails to appoint a Solicitor him or herself.

The Act also places a duties on Scottish Ministers to establish and maintain registers of individuals to act as Child Welfare Reporters, Curators ad litem and Solicitors (Section 7) and require regulations to be made about:-

(i) the requirements that a person must satisfy in order to be included and remain on the registers;

(ii) the process for including a person on and removing a person from the registers;

(iii) the process of how and by whom a registered person is to be selected as the appointed Child Welfare Reporter, Curator ad litem or Section 7 Solicitor in the case;

(iv) the remuneration of Child Welfare Reporters, Curators ad litem and Section 7 Solicitors, including expenses and outlays; and

(v) the operation and management of the three registers.

The rational is the establishment of such registers will ensure that the Child Welfare Reporters , Curators ad litem and Section 7 Solicitors are sufficiently trained. Consultation Papers were issued by the Government in March 2021. It is noted that in relation to Child Welfare Reporters and Curators ad litem, the practice of appointment varies from Sheriff Court to Sheriff Court.

It is envisaged that the registers will take time to set up. It was hoped that the Scottish Government would lay regulations before Parliament. It was the intention of the Scottish Government for the three registers to become operational from April 2023. That has not occurred and, at present, there is no indication when these registers will become operational.

Alternative Dispute Resolution (Section 23)

Section 23 of the Act requires Scottish Ministers to make funding available for alternative dispute resolution where a Section 11 order is being sought or is likely to be sought if it is not resolved through alternative dispute resolution. The Government are to set up a scheme or arrange for assistance to be made available from the Scottish Legal Aid Fund so that individuals can meet the cost of alternative dispute resolution. The Act requires the Ministers to state when they expect to fulfil the duty to set up the assistance scheme. Based on information published by the Scottish Government as of May 2022, it was envisaged that it would take another two years before it is operational. This has not occurred. The Government indicated that a priority requires to be given to addressing issues which have arisen from covid 19. They have also indicated that prior to advancing and progressing matters further, a number of matters require to be considered by the Government, including:-

- options for establishing the scheme;
- eligibility criteria;
- considering how to ensure the voice of a child is heard in ADR;
- ensuring that domestic abuse victims are not forced to attend alternative dispute resolution;
- speak to the providers of the various forms of ADR on the scheme;
- speak to the Scottish Courts and Tribunal Services on the practicalities of setting up the scheme;
- speak to bodies such as Scottish Women's Aid and Shared Parenting;
- considering how the new assistance scheme fits with the present Legal Aid Scheme; and
- any changes that are required to the court rules.

Taking account of the various matters that require to be addressed, including the provision of funding, it is envisaged that it is likely to be sometime before alternative dispute resolution becomes part of the court fabric in child disputes.

It is worth remembering that the provisions of the rules of court in both the Sheriff Court and Court of Session (Rule 33A.22 of the Sheriff Court Rules and Rule 49.23 of the Court of Session Rules) permits where a Section 11 order can be considered then the matter can be referred to mediation. This requires to be via an accredited mediator which is either CALM (Comprehensive Accredited Lawyer Mediators) or Family Mediation Scotland. With the introduction of the new Rules in the Sheriff Court, at the Initial and Full Case Management Hearings, parties require to address the Sheriff on a number of issues, including the suitability of the action for referral to mediation.

Pilot scheme for mandatory alternative dispute resolution (Section 24)

Whilst it would appear that ADR generally may take some time to move forward, Section 24 requires the Scottish Ministers to set up a pilot scheme of mandatory alternative dispute resolution meetings. A court would only be able to make an order under Section 11 of the 1995 Act in the pilot area if:-

(a) parties to the proceedings had attended a meeting where the options available to resolve the dispute had been explained; or

(b) were exempt from participating in the meeting.

The decision to exempt would be one for the court. However, the pilot scheme does not apply to proceedings in which there is a proven or alleged history of abuse.

The parties would not be required to attend the meeting together. Other exemptions could be set out by regulations.

Matters have not progressed as quickly as envisaged as a consequence of Covid 19 and other funding issues. The Government published an updated paper in March 2023 in which it was indicated that work on the establishment of a pilot of mandatory meetings and alternatives to court has been proceeding. Consideration is presently being given as to whether or not the details of the pilot can be set out in a Practice Note by the Sheriff Principals and if a decision is taken that the terms of the scheme could set out by way of Practice Note, it is envisaged the pilot may be able to commence at some point this year. However, if the pilot scheme cannot progress by way of a Practice Note then this would take longer given that the Parliamentary timetable would require to be adjusted to include time.

There clearly are issues to be considered but it is a positive that alternatives to court and the funding of alternative dispute resolution by way of a pilot study could progress, if not later this year at some point next year.

Child Contact Services

The Act, once in force, sets out provisions to regulate contact centres. This is set out in Section 10 of the Act which introduces a new Section 101C of the Children (Scotland) Act 1995. The Section provides for the regulation of contact centres with contact orders only taking place through a regulated contact service. There is provision where the court has ordered contact at a child contact centre. Contact can only be required to take place through a regulated contact service. The Act also provides that a Solicitor is prohibited from referring a person to an unregulated contact service and a failure to comply with that provision may be treated as professional misconduct or unsatisfactory professional conduct.

The Act gives Scottish Ministers powers to set out regulations, minimum standards in relation to accommodation and staff training that a contact service requires to meet in order to be a regulated contact service. In the event it cannot meet the standards, it would not be registered and cannot designate itself as a registered contact centre. There is provision for regulated contact services to be provided, as long as the conditions are met. In addition, Scottish Ministers have the power to appoint a body to inspect contact centres, regulate contact service providers and to ensure minimum standards at contact centres.

The Scottish Government published a consultation paper in March 2022. That consultation paper set out an indicative timetable for implementation of child contact service regulation.

As of September of last year, the Scottish Government advised that the consultation analysis work was currently underway and the Government expected to publish its final analysis report at some point this year.

The Scottish Government have indicated that implementation on a number of the 2020 Act provisions are dependent upon first having the register of Child Welfare Reporters in place. It is to be appreciated that the role of Child Welfare Reporters in court proceedings relating to children will increase with the introduction of the Act eg. in communicating decisions to a child and identifying the reasons why court orders (Section 11) are not being complied with.

It was to be envisaged that the register would have been operational by now. Based upon what the Scottish Government have presently said, the registration of Child Welfare Reporters does impact upon the implementation of the main provisions of the Act, as does funding, resources and training for Sheriffs and Judges.

However, whilst the main provisions of the Act are not yet in force, it is clear that children's views, who are significantly younger than twelve, will be taken into consideration and, in some way, the Act not coming into force immediately does permit us an opportunity to alter our views, our mind set and focus on how the views of young children are to be obtained.

Once the main provisions of the Act are in force, this will represent significant changes in how child disputes are determined and will ensure that the views of children of any age are given greater weight than as at present.

The Scottish Government has explained that regulation of Child Welfare Reporters has been delayed by budgetary constraints. The Government is of the view that this delay will impact on the timing of implementation of several other areas of the 2020 Act. The Scottish Government commented that the 2020 Act contains cross-references to the register of Child Welfare Reporters; some of the provisions may depend operationally on the register being up and running; and some of the changes planned by the 2020 Act are interlinked.

The Scottish Government gave three examples of parts of the Act they thought would be affected in this fashion:-

- The provision to help children better participate in court proceedings;

- The duty on the court to investigate when court orders are disobeyed; and

- The duty on the court in 2020 Act to consider the impact of delaying cases under the 1995 Act.

On the issue of delay in cases under the 1995 Act, it is worth noting that the new court rules, which are now in effect as from September of 2023, encourage courts to actively manage cases and will also be a means for encouraging the speedier resolution of family cases. However, at this juncture, complete implementation and introduction of the provisions of the Act still appear to be some way off.

'A Practical Guide to Confiscation and Restraint' by Narita Bahra QC, John Carl Townsend, David Winch
'A Practical Guide to the Law of Forests in Scotland' by Philip Buchan
'A Practical Guide to Health and Medical Cases in Immigration Law' by Rebecca Chapman & Miranda Butler
'A Practical Guide to Bad Character Evidence for Criminal Practitioners by Aparna Rao
'A Practical Guide to Extradition Law post-Brexit' by Myles Grandison et al
'A Practical Guide to Hoarding and Mental Health for Housing Lawyers' by Rachel Coyle
'A Practical Guide to Psychiatric Claims in Personal Injury – 2nd Edition' by Liam Ryan
'Stephens on Contractual Indemnities' by Richard Stephens
'A Practical Guide to the EU Succession Regulation' by Richard Frimston
'A Practical Guide to Solicitor and Client Costs – 2nd Edition' by Robin Dunne
'Constructive Dismissal – Practice Pointers and Principles' by Benjimin Burgher
'A Practical Guide to Religion and Belief Discrimination Claims in the Workplace' by Kashif Ali
'A Practical Guide to the Law of Medical Treatment Decisions' by Ben Troke
'Fundamental Dishonesty and QOCS in Personal Injury Proceedings: Law and Practice' by Jake Rowley
'A Practical Guide to the Law in Relation to School Exclusions' by Charlotte Hadfield & Alice de Coverley
'A Practical Guide to Divorce for the Silver Separators' by Karin Walker
'The Right to be Forgotten – The Law and Practical Issues' by Melissa Stock
'A Practical Guide to Planning Law and Rights of Way in National Parks, the Broads and AONBs' by James Maurici QC, James Neill et al
'A Practical Guide to Election Law' by Tom Tabori
'A Practical Guide to the Law in Relation to Surrogacy' by Andrew Powell
'A Practical Guide to Claims Arising from Fatal Accidents – 2nd Edition' by James Patience
'A Practical Guide to the Ownership of Employee Inventions – From Entitlement to Compensation' by James Tumbridge & Ashley Roughton
'A Practical Guide to Asbestos Claims' by Jonathan Owen & Gareth McAloon

'A Practical Guide to Stamp Duty Land Tax in England and Northern Ireland' by Suzanne O'Hara
'A Practical Guide to the Law of Farming Partnerships' by Philip Whitcomb
'Covid-19, Homeworking and the Law – The Essential Guide to Employment and GDPR Issues' by Forbes Solicitors
'Covid-19 and Criminal Law – The Essential Guide' by Ramya Nagesh
'Covid-19 and Family Law in England and Wales – The Essential Guide' by Safda Mahmood
'A Practical Guide to the Law of Unlawful Eviction and Harassment – 2nd Edition' by Stephanie Lovegrove
'Covid-19, Brexit and the Law of Commercial Leases – The Essential Guide' by Mark Shelton
'A Practical Guide to Costs in Personal Injury Claims – 2nd Edition' by Matthew Hoe
'A Practical Guide to the General Data Protection Regulation (GDPR) – 2nd Edition' by Keith Markham
'Ellis on Credit Hire – Sixth Edition' by Aidan Ellis & Tim Kevan
'A Practical Guide to Working with Litigants in Person and McKenzie Friends in Family Cases' by Stuart Barlow
'Protecting Unregistered Brands: A Practical Guide to the Law of Passing Off' by Lorna Brazell
'A Practical Guide to Secondary Liability and Joint Enterprise Post-Jogee' by Joanne Cecil & James Mehigan
'A Practical Guide to the Pre-Action RTA Claims Protocol for Personal Injury Lawyers' by Antonia Ford
'A Practical Guide to Neighbour Disputes and the Law' by Alexander Walsh
'A Practical Guide to Forfeiture of Leases' by Mark Shelton
'A Practical Guide to Coercive Control for Legal Practitioners and Victims' by Rachel Horman
'A Practical Guide to the Law of Driverless Cars – Second Edition' by Alex Glassbrook, Emma Northey & Scarlett Milligan
'A Practical Guide to TOLATA Claims' by Greg Williams
'A Practical Guide to Elderly Law – 2nd Edition' by Justin Patten
'A Practical Guide to Responding to Housing Disrepair and Unfitness Claims' by Iain Wightwick

'A Practical Guide to the Law of Bullying and Harassment in the Workplace' by Philip Hyland
'How to Be a Freelance Solicitor: A Practical Guide to the SRA-Regulated Freelance Solicitor Model' by Paul Bennett
'A Practical Guide to Prison Injury Claims' by Malcolm Johnson
'A Practical Guide to the Small Claims Track – 2nd Edition' by Dominic Bright
'A Practical Guide to Advising Clients at the Police Station' by Colin Stephen McKeown-Beaumont
'A Practical Guide to Antisocial Behaviour Injunctions' by Iain Wightwick
'Practical Mediation: A Guide for Mediators, Advocates, Advisers, Lawyers, and Students in Civil, Commercial, Business, Property, Workplace, and Employment Cases' by Jonathan Dingle with John Sephton
'The Mini-Pupillage Workbook' by David Boyle
'A Practical Guide to Crofting Law' by Brian Inkster
'A Practical Guide to the Law of Domain Names and Cybersquatting' by Andrew Clemson
'A Practical Guide to the Law of Gender Pay Gap Reporting' by Harini Iyengar
'NHS Whistleblowing and the Law' by Joseph England
'Employment Law and the Gig Economy' by Nigel Mackay & Annie Powell
'A Practical Guide to Noise Induced Hearing Loss (NIHL) Claims' by Andrew Mckie, Ian Skeate, Gareth McAloon
'An Introduction to Beauty Negligence Claims – A Practical Guide for the Personal Injury Practitioner' by Greg Almond
'Intercompany Agreements for Transfer Pricing Compliance' by Paul Sutton
'Zen and the Art of Mediation' by Martin Plowman
'A Practical Guide to the SRA Principles, Individual and Law Firm Codes of Conduct 2019 – What Every Law Firm Needs to Know' by Paul Bennett
'A Practical Guide to Adoption for Family Lawyers' by Graham Pegg
'A Practical Guide to Industrial Disease Claims' by Andrew Mckie & Ian Skeate
'A Practical Guide to Conducting a Sheriff Court Proof' by Andrew Stevenson
'A Practical Guide to Vicarious Liability' by Mariel Irvine
'A Practical Guide to Applications for Landlord's Consent and Variation of Leases' by Mark Shelton
'A Practical Guide to Relief from Sanctions Post-Mitchell and Denton' by Peter Causton

www.ingramcontent.com/pod-product-compliance
Ingram Content Group UK Ltd.
Pitfield, Milton Keynes, MK11 3LW, UK
UKHW021239300926
15471UKWH00013B/766

9 781916 698383